PREACHING FOR THE CONTEMPORARY SERVICE

Preaching for the Contemporary Service

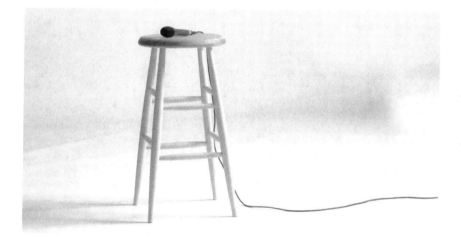

JOSEPH M. WEBB

Abingdon Press
Nashville

PREACHING FOR THE CONTEMPORARY SERVICE

This book is printed on acid-free paper.

Library of Congress Cataloging-in-Publication Data

Webb, Joseph M., 1942-
   Preaching for the contemporary service / Joseph M. Webb.
      p. cm.
   ISBN 0-687-02335-1 (pbk. : alk. paper)
   1. Preaching. I. Title.

   BV4211.3.W43 2006
   251—dc22

                                                                              2005034224

06 07 08 09 10 11 12 13 14 15—10 9 8 7 6 5 4 3 2 1

MANUFACTURED IN THE UNITED STATES OF AMERICA

CONTENTS

This book remembers two extraordinary Christians—

Bessie Webb, grandmother, always Granny. While dad was at war and mother made a living, Granny's "play church" taught two little boys the fun of worship.

Leon Appel, great preacher of the 1960s in Lincoln, Illinois. He created contemporary worship before it was called that; his joyous and biblical preaching shaped countless young lives.

PROLOGUE

On almost all occasions, the excitement begins the moment one enters the worship space. If the band is not already playing, its members are usually warming up—there is an electricity even in that. On walls, high above heads, are screens or monitors where pictures, words, and even video clips are playing. The sound system is finely tuned, and the control booths in the back are remarkably sophisticated, even in small congregations. As the service begins, the singers take their place, lyrics appear in synch with the band's building tempo, and the people, most of them young, cannot sit. There is a spontaneity even as the singing begins. No one has to call anyone to order.

For the next thirty, forty, forty-five, even fifty minutes, the people stand and sing. There is movement, even dancing, as the music turns upbeat. Sometimes the instruments are quiet and meditative; but even then the atmosphere is so charged you can feel it. Words are projected so that no one need consult a songbook or sheet. Symbolically, heads stay high, always looking up. Whether the mood is energetic, even frenetic, or subdued and taut, it is clear that the Spirit of God is in this place. Everything is alive, and while it is planned—sometimes very carefully so—it often takes on a life and a power of its own; or at least that is what its leaders hope for.

Plans can be interrupted by a testimony, or even a need that arises from within the assembled people. But nothing is to sap the spiritual, emotional, or even the intellectual energy of the time and place.

Except in a few charismatic or African American traditions, this is not your grandfather's or grandmother's worship service; it is probably not even your parents' worship service, even though many may come to enjoy this worship as much as today's young people do. This contemporary worship, sometimes called seeker's worship or digital worship, is truly revolutionary; in large part because it is making its presence felt in virtually *every* Christian denomination—liberal, conservative, mainstream, liturgical, evangelical, or free—even throughout the Roman Catholic Church. It is the free-flowing, energized liturgy of the twenty-first century.

But—when the singing stops, when the special songs have been sung, when the moving, music-backed prayers have been prayed, it is time for another staple of Christian worship, one that has been a part of every kind of worship gathering since the beginning of the church itself. It is time for the sermon. At least that is what we would say if this were a traditional worship service and not a contemporary one. Since, however, this is a contemporary worship experience and not a traditional one, are we to have a sermon? Does everything just stop now so that someone can preach for twenty or twenty-five minutes?

That, in many ways, is the great fear of today's contemporary worship planners, which is why so much literature about today's worship plays down, or even ignores, however politely, or however disguised, anything resembling a traditional sermon. The reason is clear. Traditional sermons, by reputation, are boring. They are like lectures in that they have to be endured. Even the idea of preaching conjures up, as young people know only too well, an unpleasant act through which one must occasionally suffer. And no matter how hard traditional preachers work in their traditional homiletical ways to be interesting or unusual or even cute, preaching is still dull, and not something that those who plan worship services for young people have a lot of interest in.

Some contemporary churches are lucky. They may have a really good preacher, one who is not dull, not boring, not stuck someplace in the past. They have someone who speaks with a power and energy that not only actually fits the dynamism of the music, the dancing, and the fervent prayers; but also a preacher—or speaker— who actually enhances that dynamism by the very way that he or she presents the message of the day. When that happens as part of contemporary worship, it is a profoundly thrilling experience. And one leaves the worship service hardly able to wait until the experience can be repeated.

This book contends that in the contemporary worship service there is no substitute for the preacher, the speaker, the one who stands and speaks the gospel in a dynamic, life-enhancing way. "How shall they hear without a preacher?" is still as vibrant and penetrating a question as when Paul first asked it of the new, young Roman Christians. The videos and the PowerPoint projections of the worship may help—though often they do not. Instead, as in ages past, the words of life are still carried most movingly on the wings of a passionate personality, the one who preaches the gospel message.

What does it take, though, to be the most effective preacher—or speaker—that one can be in today's contemporary worship setting? What makes the preacher's task different from what it has been for generations in traditional forms of worship? How, in short, does one become a truly effective and powerful speaker of the gospel in this energized, and energizing, atmosphere? Those are the questions that form the basis of this book.

They are also the questions now being faced by countless preachers who have spent their lives in the pulpits of traditional, usually mainstream, churches—preachers who are now faced with figuring out how to preach in new worship services that they only barely understand. They are questions being faced by young would-be preachers just entering or making their way through mainstream seminaries—hoping that they will emerge to take their places as effective preachers in today's remarkably different worship services. They are questions being faced by hopeful young preachers who have decided to skip traditional seminary educations in favor of short courses and denominational workshops that promise to give them all the training they will need to become faithful leaders and speakers in their contemporary services.

What the church at large is facing—with great difficulty—is the demand for a new kind of preacher, one well trained in the dynamic processes of public speaking, and yet with a sense of theology and practical application of the gospel. Seminaries of all denominations are playing catch up—at least the ones that recognize and are willing to confront the revolution in liturgy and worship now upon us. How is the sermon to be presented in this new environment? What is the sermon to say, and how is it to be prepared? The old ways, we are now coming to know, no longer work. Most contemporary church leaders know, too, that the powerful music and the visuals are not enough, over the long haul, to keep and feed people, young or old. In fact, today's young leaders have become aware of the revolving door effect: after having been drawn into church by the powerful music and experiential atmosphere, in time it becomes old and they drift away. This effect is the equivalent of the gospel seed falling on rocky ground and having no way to sink the roots for a plant to actually grow. Ironically, it is probably only the spoken word, the preached gospel, that can provide that soil out of which long-lasting commitments to Christ's church can actually spring up.

This book is not about the new visuals, the use of PowerPoint or movie clips. It is not about the use of new forms of music, dance, or other liturgical expression. It is not about the nature of contemporary worship or liturgy itself. There are countless new books, study guides, and helpful planning manuals concerning those things already on the market. Instead, these pages are about preaching, about the kind of preaching that contemporary worship calls for now and into the future. It is organized in a unique way, a way that runs counter to what one finds in most introductions to the art of preaching. Most of the time, the sermon process is explained in detail, including its conceptualization, scriptural basis, and organization. Finally, at the end, some words are added about delivering the sermon from the pulpit.

Not so here. Here we start with the nature of the contemporary sermon's delivery, its presentation, since in so many ways that is what makes the contemporary worship environment so different from the traditional worship setting. Then, we turn to the rules and the elements from which the contemporary sermon is actually formed, ending up with the nature of preparing the sermon itself. This does, in short, represent the logic of contemporary preaching itself. We begin, though, by asking the question, *Why preaching in contemporary worship?*

So let the new preachers, the new speakers of the Gospel message, arise. Let them learn their lessons well—not just lessons about speaking, but lessons about theology and pedagogy and in-depth Christian commitment. Let them with their new preaching raise the level of power and praise to one not achieved yet by the music and the media settings of the contemporary gospel. God will be praised through it all!

WHY PREACHING IN CONTEMPORARY WORSHIP?

Everywhere the new materials of Christian worship and liturgy tell us about what Len Wilson and Jason Moore describe as "the rise of digital culture." It is no longer the media age; it is now the digital media age. It has been seeping into our culture steadily since the 1980s, and now it has found its way into the church. "The digital deconstruction has been happening for years now, and only the most unplugged churches are unaware of the upheaval," as Wilson and Moore put it.[1] Ironically, "digital culture" is still the culture of television and other "old media," even though it is clearly new and improved and considerably expanded in both range and quality.

Writing almost thirty-five years ago, another Christian communication guru pressed the church hard to catch up with the world of global television, a world in which "the dress styles, the pop music, the politics, the hunger, the anger, and frustrations of millions of people" were all interconnected, a world that had become an "electronic 'global village.'" His name was William F. Fore, and he prophetically called the church to follow God in learning how to interact with the new forms of communication media that were just then bursting onto the scene. "God never stands still," Fore wrote in 1970:

> He is always ahead of us, speaking where we least suspect. But one thing is certain: he speaks through whatever channels are used the most, and in our time this includes the mass media of communication. This view of God's acting may be disturbing. It may require a new orientation to the media. But it is biblical. Isaiah challenged the religious people of his time to the same task: "Behold, I am doing a new thing. Even now it is springing to light. Do you not perceive it?" (Isaiah 43:18-19). Paul told the Christians at Corinth that the old had passed away, that all things have become new. It is by examining and understanding what the mass media are saying today that we can keep open to "a word from the Lord."[2]

Despite all of the foresight of William Fore and a few other media-savvy Christians who tried to get the church/media interaction underway, their words fell on deaf ears. Until the past decade or two, when a new generation began to appear. Weaned on saturation media, they were poised to either leave the church behind, or bring their media along with them into the places of worship and Christian service. God is still there, as Fore said, "always ahead of us."

What *is* truly new on the contemporary Christian scene, however—newer, in a sense, than even the technology itself—is the growing number of bright, talented young Christians who not only know media, but are not afraid to work hard at figuring out how the church should react to, interact with, and even build upon the new digital technologies. That's what was missing in Fore's day. So it is no wonder that the media revolution in Christian worship and work is finally here. No one, and nothing, will be spared its impact. More than that, it is not only here, but there is no turning back.

The dangers, though, are also clear. In their ground-breaking study, Wilson and Moore write that "many church leaders do not yet have an idea of how digital media are capable of empowering churches to transform lives with the Gospel of Jesus Christ."[3] Moreover, "the comfortable response is usually for churches to retreat to established forms of Gospel communication from an earlier era, where problems in interpretation have mostly been worked out."[4] That is not where the most severe danger lies, however. The worst danger is in not getting a clear fix on the *limitations* of digital media within the new church settings. This, of course, will take both time and experience. It will also take clearheaded, realistic thinking about how the new digital media actually impact fundamental dimensions of Christian worship, learning, experience, and collective participation.

Yes, as Wilson and Moore, along with a number of other young Christian writers on media, point out, it is necessary for the church to make the jump from old worship forms to the new ones demanded by the coming of digital media. A realistic view of this jump, however, demands that we think carefully about what the new digital media can actually provide for Christian worship, and what—again, realistically—it cannot provide.

When new church leaders like Wilson and Moore say they do not want to "retreat to established forms of Gospel communication" they mean that they want to move cleanly away from the church's traditional liturgical forms, particularly from those old traditional sermons, that old kind of preaching, the preaching that has, with exceptions, been dull, generally lifeless, unchallenging, and often difficult to listen to. Granted, a lot of older people grew up with worship and preaching styles that they just got used to and never left behind. But even when the now aging baby boomers reached adulthood in the 1960s—William Fore among them—the church's worship, and particularly its preaching, was becoming increasingly difficult to bear. It is not coincidental that during the 1970s and 1980s came the decline in church membership and attendance across almost all mainline denominations.

At a certain point, however, a resurgence began. New worship forms, characterized largely by the new music styles and the informalities of both dress and hierarchy, began to appear. The influence of so-called charismatic churches, with their high emotionalism, caught on around the fringes of numerous established denominations. New fast-growing, media-tuned churches began to appear. The old liturgical forms were being disposed of. One of those old forms was the sermon.

But what about the sermon? Even now the developers of today's contemporary worship are not at all sure what to do with it any more than most traditional preachers are sure what to do with contemporary worship. On one hand, the young (and young at heart) contemporary worship developers know that preaching is as old as the church itself. They also know that the church would not have even come into existence without preaching. Yet they also know, or believe, that few things over the past half century have more undermined the church's life, vitality, and appeal than the lifeless preaching that has flowed from countless pulpits, both Protestant and Catholic.

At the very heart of the contemporary worship is not just the introduction of new music or the imposition of new informalities—at its very core is a profound and unmistakable critique of the sermon. Yes, preaching is important, most young contemporary church leaders would say, and there are, without question, some great preachers out there. But if traditional preaching is all there is, then new leaders say that preaching can have no long-term, viable place in the contemporary worship service.

For example, in their *Fresh Out of the Box* books, Len Wilson, Jason Moore, Amelia Cooper Boomershine, and Tom Boomershine point out that they want to provide "direction for experiencing the scripture firsthand, rather than through a detached analysis of its theological, doctrinal meaning."[5] In *Digital Storytellers*, Len Wilson and Jason Moore say that contemporary worship is based on "experience, rather than meaning,"[6] and that the new digital media that

4

provide the basis for the new generation's worship "prefers interactivity to passivity."[7] Elsewhere they note that contemporary worship's orientation is designed to provide a "holistic picture of the Gospel, which goes beyond a lesson-of-the-day mentality."[8]

There is a powerful and biting critique of what they have heard in the preaching of the traditional churches. In too much of it, the scriptures are not experienced firsthand, analysis is detached, the preacher is concerned only with correct meaning and not with creating experience as a result of the preaching itself. Most telling, perhaps, is the idea that the preaching leaves congregants passive, since they have not been engaged in any kind of interactive participation. Then there is the lesson-of-the-day mentality, a kind of ho-hum attitude toward the gospel rather than turning Holy Scripture into a living, breathing, dynamic Word from God.

Everything in this list we take up in this book. We listen. We take seriously this new vision of preaching for contemporary worship. Our cues are there. There is no disputing the notion that traditional preaching has not only left much to be desired; but it has effectively alienated a whole generation of bright young people from the church's traditional life. Now those young people are demanding not just something different, but something better. It is not preaching that is the problem. It is ineffective preaching. That can be changed, though—and it must be.

The danger lies in thinking that preaching can be done away with in the contemporary church. It cannot be. Not just because it is preaching, but because preaching, the public speaking of the gospel, embodies the human personality passionately reaching out to other human personalities. That is not just the way of the gospel. It is the way of God's human creation. Certain things can be mediated and even experienced indirectly. But the really important things cannot be.

To be fair, in their books and CDs for worship Wilson and Moore include a short section with each worship outline that they label simply "Integration." It is usually a couple of paragraphs discussing a biblical text and even its use. Here is the opening paragraph of one, for example, which uses the movie on the flight of Apollo 13 to construct a service titled, "The Difference a Day Makes":

> The New Testament contains a story of two Peters. The Peter of the Gospels is a regular dude—a fisherman, who loved the sea, loved being a guy, acted impulsively and alternately with or without courage. But Acts shows a very different Peter—one who has the authority and leadership to guide the fledgling church to its future. The character of his change personifies the power of the resurrection that is expressed at Pentecost. The resurrected Jesus had transformed Peter's life. In fact, his change is in some ways the strongest empirical evidence of the fact of the Resurrection, for those looking for evidence for their faith.[9]

These comments are intended to be speaking notes, or even sermon notes, for someone who might speak during this highly visual, music- and even comedy-filled contemporary service. The short Integration section, however, has nothing about format or use surrounding it; they are textual notes with a bit of explanation and application that could easily evolve into a sermon of some kind. The notes are intended, the authors say, to "identify clues in the text about the dynamics of the original telling and hearing of the story itself." Worship leaders are then told to "develop these ideas in whatever way will be most helpful to your congregation."[10]

So the preacher speaking is gingerly made a part of contemporary worship. In fact, at the beginning of each of the *Fresh Out of the Box* books the same words about public speaking in contemporary worship are repeated: "In public speaking, studies have shown that when the people are 'lost' to the message, it takes 20 minutes or more to bring them back. Further, we live in a non-linear world. Thus we are used to 'multi-tasking,' engaging in multiple stimuli at once." The writers, though, are not trying to provide some insight into a preaching mode, but simply urging that in contemporary worship one must "fill the gaps between the listed elements" of the service.[11] In other words, everything in the service must segue

together as seamlessly as possible, since in the media world that sur-
rounds us, we are not used to breaks, which can easily turn into
dead time or space.

Still, in these statements from the Wilson and Moore books, a
subtle orientation to preaching exists. What is called for in the
contemporary worship setting is not just better preaching. It is a
different kind of preaching than has generally existed before; or
that has existed in the worship outposts of mainline denominations; and one can, without question, find manifestations of it
through various evangelical and even fundamentalist churches.
Now, though, it is a kind of preaching that must not only be understood but embraced for a new time and place—and a new generation; and mainline seminaries, charged with teaching future
preachers to preach, have to learn to teach it.

The preacher for contemporary worship must learn to speak
experientially, inspirationally, creatively, and passionately—in a
dynamic style that is both participatory and interactive. Those are
the new, explicit base criteria. But this description is more than just
a style of public address. This approach to preaching, or speaking,
will profoundly involve both what is said by the preacher as well as
how he or she prepares for speaking. All of it—as we shall see in
this book—is a part of the same new fabric.

We still, though, have not answered the most basic question.
What is there about preaching, or public speech in worship, that
requires it to stay at or near the center of contemporary worship?
What is there about this human contact of one person speaking
before a crowd of persons that even the recent emergence of new
visual media cannot, in the end, surpass?

There are three distinct ways of answering that question.

The first is that an animated, informed, passionate speaker, one
who speaks with empathy, caring, and insight, creates one of the
most potent forms of human *experience* imaginable. That presumes
not just that the speaker is a good one, and that she or he is speaking on a matter of great interest to those who listen to the speech.

When those factors come together, though, a public speaker can mesmerize an audience, just as a great singer or other performer can. We have all heard speakers who can hold us spellbound for long stretches of time. There are ways to do this, and one of the purposes of this book is to explain how it can be accomplished on a regular basis—as it should be in the contemporary worship service.

There is another way, though, to look at this issue. Think about the difference between someone *on stage*, whether a band, a singer, or some other kind of performer, or even a public speaker—with that same performer's or speaker's image projected on a large screen above the performer. Let's say it's a great standup comic, like a Jerry Seinfeld. One buys a ticket, but when one gets to the arena, Seinfeld is not there, but, "fortunately," we are told, he will be performing live in New York, and will be seen "live" on the large screen in place on the stage. We are further told that the live TV medium is very powerful, so one will not miss any of the flavor or the nuance of Seinfeld's performance; he is, after all, performing live someplace in New York, and we are getting to watch it via the magic of satellite. He performs and there is laughter, as one would expect at seeing something on a big screen TV, and even some scattered applause.

Then imagine, though, that right in the middle of the big screen TV performance, from off in the wings Jerry Seinfeld himself emerges and takes the stage. What would the reaction be? The response would be wildly overwhelming. He is *here*, in person, not live on TV, but live right here on stage. We are in the same room with him. We are breathing the same air, right now. If we walked up there, we could shake hands.

As wonderful as the giant screens are, with their close-up clips and their words and their sincerely delivered messages, there is nothing like a real person down there, or up there. A real presence in this very place, or on this very platform has an experiential power that no medium in the same space can match. We pay our money to go to movies, of course; and when we know that is what we are going to see, we gladly accept what we get. But it is really something special, and something for which we will pay dearly, when we know we are going to get to see someone, or hear someone or some group—and we are going to see and hear him or her live. A TV screen onstage is interesting and sometimes remarkably powerful; but a real person, able to speak well, is almost always a much more potent experience on that stage.

The second way to answer the question about the importance of effective preaching in contemporary worship arises from what every great teacher knows firsthand. It is that human speech, coming from a savvy, informed, and deeply caring teacher—i.e., speaker— is the most potent mode of formation and persuasion there is. We have all experienced it in our own lives. In our growing up, the moments that have changed us, that have pointed in an unforgettable direction, that have provided us with a breakthrough insight, have almost all come from a teacher or mentor who took the time to talk to us; often privately, but surprisingly often, in the midst of a profoundly moving class lecture or discussion.

The right question was asked (and maybe we had to answer it for ourselves); a challenge was articulated; a passing comment was made that clicked on a lightbulb in our head. There was often a visual aid nearby—good teachers always seemed to have them handy—but it was invariably what that teacher *said* that stuck; and one of the major reasons it did was because of who said it, and who we were at the moment it was said. It was a real caring person who spoke, and it made all the difference in the world.

On the other side of that coin, any teacher who has been at it a long time knows how speaking the right words—often unplanned words, with a small group of students, or even in front of a large class—can impact student lives. A film may be shown that captures attention or raises awareness; but the teacher knows very well that the power of the film will invariably be lodged in what the teacher says, or leads the students to say, after the film is over.

The teacher also knows that when materials get a bit complicated or abstract only one thing can suffice to carry the student successfully through; and that is the careful, often slightly repetitious *explanation* that comes from the teacher's own lips.

No matter how digital or esoteric, the one thing that media do not do very well is explain things. Not even magazines or books do that very well. Answering the basic, *What does that mean?* or *How does this work?* questions invariably require not just the hands, but even more important, the voice of the teacher.

"It works like this," and then comes the demonstration, along with the kind and careful words of the one who knows what or how. Anyone who has ever tried to follow the written directions for putting together, say, a bicycle knows how wonderful it would be to have someone nearby to explain how to read and understand the directions themselves. If we had that, we all seem to know, there would not be as many pieces left over when we finally have constructed what looks like a bicycle. Sometimes now, too, we get a videotaped or DVD set of directions; and while they are better, there is no way to use our facial expressions to express our inability to follow where the smooth teacher could take us ever so quickly.

From the classroom experience comes one other important understanding. Invariably, too, when we find ourselves having been persuaded of something, when our opinion about something has become clearer or stronger, it is because we have listened to someone that we trust talking about it. We listen—we like to listen, despite our being told how badly we do it. We seldom read things that actually persuade us to change our views. We very seldom see something on television or in a movie—even when it might be played in church—that persuades us to a new orientation or idea. We may become fascinated, or even captivated; and while we may sometimes be influenced, we seldom are actually persuaded. But let someone have a serious talk with us, and, depending on who it is and what the situation is, some serious persuasion can take place in our minds and hearts.

The third important thing about the need for public speaking, or good preaching, in contemporary worship has to do with the fact that the very act of *empowerment* or *commissioning* can usually only be done by a passionate human person and voice. The church, whatever its form, is to function as a servant in the world. Worship is important. It is the offering of oneself to God. It is one's expression of praise to God, the Creator, Redeemer, and Life Giver. In all of these things, though, worship has never been historically conceived as only an end in itself. It is always also the preparation for sending Christ's servants out as light and salt into the world.

"As you go into all the world," was the Great Commission of Christ to his disciples; and by implication and extension to us as well. So how and where is that Commission given its verbal expression and activation? How are people sent? How are we sent? We are sent through the passionate words of the one who embodies the living voice of Jesus Christ within worship, in contemporary worship, a voice of commissioning to Christ's work today. But commissions always in turn require—as the ancient church put it—the laying on of hands. While that can be quite literal, it is also another way of saying that the sending requires real people, speaking real words, in the midst of real believers. The speaking of words—powerful, eternal, biblical words of testimony—is part and parcel with that laying on of hands. One comes to worship in order to be sent back out, to carry out the day-to-day work of "being Christ" among hungry, hurting, lost people.

In short, the voice of the preacher, alive, energetic, clear and contemporary, must not fade from today's dynamic new forms of worship—contemporary forms that are already shaping the coming generations. How will these new preachers, with passionate new words for new generations, do their work? This book sets out to propose what contemporary preaching will need to be like in order to take its rightful place in the midst of these dynamic and bustling congregations of the young and the young at heart.

Notes

1. Len Wilson and Jason Moore, *Digital Storytellers: The Art of Communicating the Gospel in Worship* (Nashville: Abingdon Press, 2002), 14.

2. William F. Fore, *Image and Impact: How Man Comes Through in the Mass Media* (New York: Friendship Press, 1970), 12-13.

3. Wilson and Moore, 15.

4. Ibid., 14.

5. Len Wilson, Jason Moore, Amelia Cooper Boomershine, and Tom Boomershine, *Fresh Out of the Box, Vol. 1: Digital Worship Experiences for Palm Sunday Through Pentecost Sunday* (Nashville: Abingdon Press, 2002), 14.

6. Len Wilson and Jason Moore, *Digital Storytellers: The Art of Communicating the Gospel in Worship* (Nashville: Abingdon Press, 2002), 21. They say it this way: "The church must make the jump from modern formulas for ministry to the postmodern, or more accurately digital, forms if it expects to reach the culture of the digital age. Worship can and will become rooted in digital culture forms but continue to reinvigorate the traditions that have come before us. This transition in digital culture is based upon experience, rather than meaning."

7. Ibid., 29.

8. Ibid., 163.

9. *Fresh Out of the Box*, Vol. 1, 90.

10. Ibid., 14.

11. Ibid., 6.

CHAPTER ONE

CONTEMPORARY PREACHING AS IMPROVISATION

T here is not a preacher anywhere, of whatever age, denomination, or theological inclination, who does not long to create a religious experience, an experience centered in God, every time he or she takes to the pulpit or platform. It is not unlike the baseball batter who, deep down, longs to hit a home run every time he or she steps to the plate, whether it is the bottom of the ninth or not. "May this sermon move people, lift them to new heights, empower them in an unforgettable way": that is the lofty, silent, prayerful longing, however inarticulated, of every preacher before every sermon—from the young, eager newcomer who simply plans to do that, to the experienced preacher who has long ago given up on the idea that it is even possible to preach with such an effect.

People come to church literally hungry for that experience, that sense of being profoundly moved, inspired. They hope for it not just from the music, from the surroundings, and from the lively sense of participation; they also hope for it from the one who speaks God's Word, the preacher. They express that intense need in a variety of ways. A recent study, funded by the Lilly Endowment and extending over several years, conducted interviews with dozens and dozens of church lay people about what they thought about the preachers and the preaching they listened to. One of the most important and consistent aspects of the interviews is the way almost everyone interviewed tried, without knowing how, to get preachers to take the creation of that experience in the sermon seriously.

Anthony, for example, explained what he wanted the experience of the sermon to be like:

> It touches your heart. . . . It touches my heart when it touches my inner self, my inner feelings. . . . I consider myself a strong person, but also an emotional person to the degree of letting someone else say something that will touch me. You grow up. You're out there between streets and church and activity outside of church that you have to grow up in. I just don't let everybody touch my feelings. It's very important to me when the pastor has the ability to do that. It's almost like the words that he says, he just touched your hand and go right through you.[1]

Or look at this brief part of an interview with Cassandra who was asked if there was ever a time she wanted to walk out of a church service. After saying "yes, there were some times that she wanted to," she told this story that captures the importance of that special experience of engagement in a different way:

> A lady . . . came to me and said, "I want you to know I'm leaving the church." I go, "Why?" She said, "I'm not getting anything out of the sermons." . . . It can happen that the sermons don't engage you, and if you're not engaged, then you don't get anything out of it. Then you go, "I need to go somewhere else. I need to seek." I can only speak for myself; I do come seeking some sense of fulfillment, and I guess my expectation is I'm coming with my cup empty now and I need a little something in my cup.[2]

There is no question that in today's contemporary worship service, it is absolutely necessary to have preaching that touches people, that profoundly inspires them, that makes something happen in their hearts and minds and beings. But what is inspiration, or experience? What does it mean? How does a preacher, any preacher, achieve that in preaching the Word? Can any preacher, young or old, learn to preach in a way that keeps people, particularly young people, *wanting* to come to church?

The answer this book gives to that question is an unqualified yes—preachers, no matter how old or how young, can preach in a way that creates an unforgettable inspirational experience of God. But that word, *experience*, as good and useful as it is, is very complicated. We realize that the minute we try to define it.

Experience is, in fact, a very sensory word. It involves our senses. In its most basic form, it refers to things that arise out of the hardscrabble living of our lives. It encompasses things that we see, hear, and touch, and even, in extraordinary situations, taste, smell, and absorb. Our bodies and everything in us react to what we go through; nothing about us is unaffected. Our minds, our emotions, our instincts, our hearts and souls and spirits are all affected by what we go through every day that we live—the good, the bad, the hard, the painful, the joyful, the times when we pushed the bottom and lifted to the heights. This is experience. We need to speak, or shout, or sing, or cry, or laugh; or do any number of things in response to the experiences in which we find ourselves. It is true that in most preaching situations, we are usually fairly quiet, listening intently; it is also true that when the preacher does touch us, or call out things in us, or cause us to be caught up in something very special, something in us can cry out or react in some other unplanned manner—and this is not just in the call-and-response preaching of African American traditions. In deeply moving experiences, we can react physically and often vocally; we do, in fact, find any number of ways, sometimes subtle, sometimes overt, to turn our stirred senses loose in response to a moving, dynamic sermon.

In short, to experience something, anything, is to become totally caught up in it, literally consumed by it for a time; it is to participate in it to the fullest and deepest of one's capacities—sensually, emotionally, and mentally. It is to shut out, even forget, everything else going on. It is to become lost in the experience itself—not in a drifting sort of way, or even necessarily in something trancelike; but in a completely engaged and concentrated way.

So how can a public speaker—the preacher—standing alone before a congregation, create that unforgettable experience of faith or experience of God for everyone in the congregation? It can be done, and anyone who desires it more than anything else and who is willing to learn the basics of contemporary public speech can do it. It requires, too, a willingness to put one's preaching in God's hands, seeking the Holy Spirit's permeation of the process as well. It requires, as we shall see, letting one's preaching arise from the pages of the Holy Bible, at the same time connecting with imagination and creativity to people in the present. But it can be done by anyone with an ambition to preach the gospel in a new way in a new world.

Experience and Improvisational Drama

What is that new way for a new world? As much as some veteran preachers do not want to acknowledge it, to stand in front of people to speak is to be part of one of the oldest art forms known to humans: the art of performance. For some in the church, to talk about preaching as performance is uncomfortable. Performance is artificial. Not so, however. As Viola Spolin, one of the masters of the modern theatre, has put it, "the techniques of the theatre are the techniques of communicating."[3]

Theatre, like other forms of art, has always been about the creating of experience, with all of the breadth and depth that we can pack into that extraordinary word. The goal of those who stand on

16

the stage or platform is to carry the audience away, out of themselves, to places they have been never been, to where they once were but would like to go again, up and beyond the restricted confines of their own lives. The goal is to imbue the audience with spirits from other places, from above, spirits that they wish to know but have difficulty conjuring up on their own. The goal is to bring the unseen depths that hide within every audience member to the surface where possibilities can be seen, examined, and reveled in. This requires great preparation, involvement, and energy from the one who stands on the stage or platform. This is a remarkable opportunity and responsibility—and it is always very hard work. It is not only the work of the actor; it is also the work of the preacher, the one who stands to speak the gospel of the Living God.

The stage, the platform, the pulpit, is a living, dynamic place. All of the senses of both the speaker and the audience, the congregation, are to be engaged. This is not just theatre. This is divine theatre. This is the place where Christian experience will be conjured up and made immediate, where something from beyond will take place. It will also be the place where those who share the experience will be remade, re-formed, moved to higher ground. It will also be the place from where minds, hearts, and spirits will experience and act in the world in a different way, a way motivated by a new sense of Christ living within us all.

It is not just the liturgy that creates a sense of the holy for the congregation. The speaking of the gospel must create it as well. Here there will be comedy, tragedy, pathos, suffering, and triumph. Here there will—in the speaking of the gospel—be absolute quiet, a divine stillness, as well as boisterous rejoicing, a breaking through of angelic noise. This is drama of the highest order. The experiences are not artificial; they are real. The inspiration that flows in and through these experiences is not fleeting; it energizes every person throughout the living of ordinary days.

This is the contemporary worship experience—and preaching the gospel, meaning vibrant, dynamic public address from the platform, is not just a part of the experience; in many ways, it is the center of the experience. As we consider *how* to do it, as we must, we start with its dramatic roots: there we shall learn our fundamental lessons of method. We keep in mind, too, what Spolin said about theatre: "The actuality of the communication is far more important than the method used. Methods alter to meet the needs of time and place." [4] We are speaking now, though, of our time and place; and even as we keep method in perspective, without it, there can be no inspirational experience.

With that in mind, we turn to the dynamics of theatre itself as our guide. There are two basic categories of performance drama. The first is scripted drama; or, in our case, scripted public speech. This includes the learning and performance of plays or monologues. The words and often the stage directions are provided for the actors, who must infuse both with meaning and emotion. When this is done well, of course—and it is not easy to do, as anyone who has acted in a school play can attest—then the words, characters, and plots are brought vividly to life. Becoming a professional actor or actress requires an extraordinary amount of talent, training, and experience—as any good stage or screen performer learns.

The other kind of drama is *improvised*. Ironically, it was probably the original form of acting or public performance, with a general idea proposed or worked out, with the action and dialogue more or less improvised as the characters went along. Today, improvisational theatre is much more than a respected theatrical art form; it is also the basis for virtually all of the new television "reality" shows, with (at least in theory) the scripts and the prepackaged plots rejected in favor of a "going where this takes us" type of show. This is to say nothing, of course, about the best known and most widespread kind of improv—the stand-up comedy performances of A&E's "An Evening at the Improv," or the countless comedy stand-ups of the Comedy Channel.

In this model of public speaking, the stand-up performer or player takes to the stage alone with nothing more than a pencil-thin microphone, and he or she speaks to an audience of paying customers for up to an hour. This speaking is done in such a way that they believe they have gotten their money's worth in whatever kind of laughter and whimsy the speaker conjures up with nothing more than a voice, a persona, and an occasional prop. It is a daunting task, to say the least—and yet that is what improv, including improvisational public speaking at its very highest is expected to achieve.

Different improv artists treat the process differently, of course; some tell jokes, which is itself not an art for amateurs, since the tendency of jokes is to fall flat. Jokes are seldom funny in themselves; how they are told makes them funny. Others tell stories, most often stories from real life, from the foibles of language and behavior that beset us all; and our laughter, interlaced sometimes with tears, is laughter at ourselves. Still others do not set out to be funny at all; they will come at us, in a sense, with the mirror of truth, and we will cringe and reflect and feel deeply; and be grateful that we have together shared deeply important things.

This stand-up improvisation, with both men and women as the speakers, and with crowds willing to purchase tickets to take part, tells us that improvisational public speaking—with its blend of comic entertainment, social commentary, and sheer wit—is the highest form of public address available to us. It is improvisational theatre, part acting, part conversation with the audience, part just talking, that points us toward the kind of public speaking that best interfaces with the gospel in today's contemporary worship.

So—what is improvisation? It is not just anything that happens, or anything that someone does, since it always involves rules and boundaries. By its very nature, though, improv is always unscripted. Yet it is not made up as one goes along, not off the cuff, since everything is always done within some framework of order, logic, and preparation. It is, on the other hand, the art of the unexpected, a free play of artistic expression. Improv is planned in the sense of being based on certain disciplines; but, in its fullest sense, it is unplanned in the sense of not progressing as a fully scripted undertaking. At its best, improv delights in surprise and risk. It is about people being themselves, doing what they would always do—or never do. There is, without question, something profoundly compelling about such live performance.

Every great human art form has its improvisational dimension; more accurately, its improvisational foundation. In painting, for example, the great German expressionist Wassily Kandinsky created countless influential canvases composed of lines, shapes and colors, most of which he called "improvisations." It is not an exaggeration to say that the freedom with which he painted the human inner world set the stage for much twentieth century art. Jazz is the music of improvisation in its myriad legendary expressions, including those that go back even to the classical musicians and composers. From the astonishing bands of Bourbon Street to the elegant and popular horn and piano jazz stylists to the scat singers who followed the incomparable Ella Fitzgerald, virtually no musical form has been unaffected by jazz improvisation. In the theatre, improvisation has long been a staple, dating from the Greeks through the Shakespearean era to the modern media forms. From all quarters, the sense of improvisation is the same: it is the most dangerous as well as the most vulnerable kind of art—but it is also the most engaging, stirring the spirit and energizing the heart.

We Live Improvisationally

Whatever its expression, improvisation essentially reflects the art of living itself. In other words, we all know implicitly and intuitively what improv is: it is what we do every day without knowing it. In that sense, it is the art of the human soul. We make our decisions day in and day out improvisationally. We plan as carefully as we can, but in our actual living, in moving through any given day trying to follow through on our plans, everything—literally everything—turns into an improvisational situation. We try to control the situations in which we find ourselves, only to discover how seldom we can ever actually do that. So we take what comes, rolling with the punches, improvising all the way. A restaurant doesn't have wheat bread for a sandwich today—so what do we do? We comb the menu. We will improvise and end up with something we had not planned on. Someone is late for a meeting, so we improvise. The car breaks down at a most inconvenient time, so we improvise. Improvisation is not only who we are; it shapes who we are. That is one of the basic reasons why we like to see good improvisation from others: we not only identify with it, we learn from it.

Our actual living emerges on its own terms, filled with tensions over which we try always to maintain a certain amount of control. Thus, our lives become comic masterpieces of playing, running frantically about, trying to keep track of objects and other people, such as kids, parents, and work colleagues; we labor to get to where we are supposed to be on time, and then make up excuses when we are late. Improvise, improvise, improvise—it never stops. In a remarkable little book titled, *Free Play: Improvisation in Life and Art*, Stephen Nachmanovitch explores in a delightful way this improvisational mainspring of all human life:

> A creative life is risky business. To follow your own course, not patterned on parents, peers, or institutions, involves a delicate balance of tradition and personal freedom, a delicate balance of sticking to your guns and remaining open to change. While on some dimensions living a normal life, you are nevertheless a pioneer, venturing into new territory, breaking away from the molds and models that inhibit the heart's desire, creating life as it goes. Being, acting, creating in the moment without props and supports, without security, can be supreme play, and it can also be frightening, the very opposite of play. Stepping into the unknown can lead to delight, poetry, invention, humor, lifetime friendships, self-realization, and occasionally a great creative breakthrough.[5]

We literally live improvisationally. When we get up in the morning, even if no one else is in the house, we begin the day in an improvisational manner. We have habits or routines, of course; we could not make it without them. Yet even within those routines we say things in ways that we have never said them before. We make it up as we go along, and this is particularly true if anything happens to break our morning pattern.

Someone calls with news; and we improvise as we respond to an unfolding and unrehearsed conversation. A kitty is sick when we get up, or perhaps we have been awakened by a pet in distress; and we have to improvise how to respond to an unexpected, and even distressing, situation. Our improvisation itself has to be constantly shifted, since we are frustrated in our first attempts to respond to the unexpected situation. We make a phone call, and no one answers, or someone answers who cannot help us, but who makes some suggestions. We improvise some breakfast, depending on how much time we have to do it; we improvise some fast e-mail messages, replying hurriedly to some overnight notes that were left for us. We are off to work, and traffic is such that we have to improvise on how to keep the trip from becoming longer than we want it to be. At work, conversations and situations of every kind, many of them unplanned and unprepared for, await us; and, with every skill we can muster, we *improvisationally* talk our way through them. With a few friends in the evening, around a dinner table or at a nice restaurant that we all like, the talk is lively and filled with fun—with every bit of it fully and dynamically improvised as it progresses through to day's end.

Strangely, no one actually teaches us how to improvise. It seems to be in our very nature as social human beings. Improvisation provides the fabric not only for almost all of our dealings with other people, family, friends, colleagues, and strangers alike, but also we constantly work to get people in our lives to do what we want them to do; and often they are strikingly resistant to many of our efforts. It is almost like they are trying, either singly or in groups, to get us to do what they want us to do; and the result is not unlike a contest of improvisational wits and skills. Nothing is more instructive for someone who wants to become an expert at improvisational public speaking than to become acutely conscious of the dynamics of normal daily improvised interaction. Think about the day-to-day living subject matter that turns so utterly hilarious in the hands of a great stand-up comic.

Removing the Fourth Wall

When life and improvisation move to the stage or the platform, it truly becomes something very special. It becomes drama without what in legitimate theatre is called the *fourth wall*. In the world of theatre, whether on proscenium arched stage or even in the round, the fourth wall separates the actors from the audience. This means that the performance goes on as though no one else is even present; actors onstage are not so much as to even look at someone or something in the audience. Only the world of the stage actually exists to the performers. Occasionally, a play will be written that intentionally violates that rule—as it does with the role of the stage manager in Thornton Wilder's great play, *Our Town*; but even then only *that* character is given permission to talk with the audience—and only then in character.

In improv stand-up comedy, however, the rule is changed. That separating fourth wall is taken down so that the speaker is placed in a *face-to-face position* with the audience. While improvisationally the speaker does "perform," it is understood that the speaker is himself or herself (however that might actually be modified); and that the interactions with the audience are genuine and, to whatever extent the speaker wishes, are an integral part of the performance itself. It is fully *participatory* theatre. The very nature of that speaker-audience interaction means that the speaker, by removing the fourth wall, cannot *ever* fully control what or how the audience members may, on their own, contribute to the performance. That, in a real sense, is where the true nature of improv public speech can be seen.

What is there, though, about improvisational public speaking, the kind the stand-up comedian does, that carries such enormous appeal—and makes it the public speaking model for touching and moving people? There are three or four characteristics that give improvisational speech a strangely unique power that kicks in when one person uses it onstage, or on a worship platform, or in a church pulpit. They are its inherent intimacy, its ability to be totally spontaneous, its vivacious energy, and what we will call its nature as *monological dialogue*, or we can turn the words around and call it a *dialogical monologue*. Briefly, we need to touch on each of these characteristics.

The Intimacy of Improvisation

Improvisation is motion; it is movement. It is looking at people, here, there, wherever they are, and carrying on a running conversation with them. Sometimes it is inviting them to talk back to you, not in an ongoing stream, since the relations between speaker and audience have to be maintained. But it is direct communication of the kind that goes on between or among friends. When the dynamics of good public speaking, using natural eye contact, gestures, and body movements, are practiced, and when the speaker makes an effort to reach out, often quite literally, to the audience or congregation, the result is that every person present feels that the speaker is looking directly at, and even talking directly to, him or her—an experience that everyone who has ever listened to a great professional speaker (or preacher) has had.

Strangely, this was put as vividly as I have ever seen it in the preaching interview with Albert that we referred to at the beginning of this chapter. Albert was asked what he would like to see in a preacher when the preacher is preaching. He said he liked to see movement, both hand movements and walking around. He said movement keeps people focused on what the preacher is saying.

That's an apt description of how intimacy works in public speaking. It is a remarkable sense of there being only two people in the room—the speaker and each one who is there. Hundreds can be present, and yet that same quality of one-on-one intimacy is achievable; but it is only possible when the speaker has every dimension of human contact focused and in place—from unrelenting eye movement to hand and arm gestures, to literal movement about the space, to a reaching out with voice, inflection, tone, and pauses. It represents the fundamentals of public speaking, carried to their highest and most concentrated use. Ironically, what results from this kind of improvisational speech is not a big, fill-the-house speech, but a small, whispered speech, with the lows as important as the highs; what results is an intimate encounter in which every single person is touched by what has taken place among even a vast number of people.

The Spontaneity of Improvisation

The digital world is a spontaneous world; or it may be that our world has become so planned and regimented that we hunger day in and day out for something, anything, to be spontaneous. *Spontaneous*, of course, means unplanned, unscripted, unpremeditated, having an unknown outcome. It is ironic in our time, too, to have a new television genre known as the reality show, which is nothing more than a feeble effort to create spontaneous television. Put people, often ordinary people, in very unordinary and often unhuman situations and see how they will react. Turn on the cameras and let's watch. Let's have a program in which we don't know how it will end—and we will let the audience come along for that very "spontaneous" ride.

25

Obviously, improvisation has at its very heart the drive of spontaneity. It is spontaneity onstage or on the platform, whether it is the group spontaneity of actors bouncing off of each other in an unscripted fashion, or a single person onstage bouncing off of the audience in the manner of a stand-up comic. Spolin has written that

> Through spontaneity we are re-formed into ourselves. It creates an explosion that for the moment frees us from handed-down frames of reference, memory choked with old facts and information and undigested theories and techniques of other people's findings. Spontaneity is the moment of personal freedom when we are faced with a reality and see it, explore it and act accordingly. In this reality the bits and pieces of ourselves function as an organic whole. It is the time of discovery, of experiencing, of creative expression. [6]

What does that mean? It means at least two things that are important for us. First, it means that spontaneity is freedom. Not the freedom to do anything that we wish, as important as that can be; but the freedom to be fully and truly ourselves onstage, in front of and with people. In fact, it is the freedom to be what those who come to see us or hear us expect and want us to be; not based on expectations from the past, or expectations formed by outside influences even. But based on who are we and what are we—and how we became this kind of person. That's what she means by spontaneity being a means for re-forming ourselves.

Ironically, this is as true of improvisation in contemporary worship as it is for improv in the theatrical, or stand-up, setting. That is, people who come to church to hear the improvisational preacher want him or her to be fully and truly himself or herself. They want that preacher to put aside the prepared stuff, the preprogrammed expectations, and just talk to us, be real with us, and let us see and experience who you, the preacher or the message bringer, really are.

The second thing it means is that in this improvisational openness there is a chance, often a long shot but a chance nevertheless, that something remarkably creative and life-changing may actually take place. This is what Spolin means by calling the improv moment a "time of discovery." There is no way to plan to be creative—every artist of any stripe knows that; and the Lord knows that every artist has tried. One cannot make discovery happen; if so, we would all be well-known discoverers of things. No, one can only set up conditions, as it were, situations in which something might happen that had not taken place before, or something new might be found, or come into being or whatever. Invariably, the conditions for creation, for discovery, or even for experiencing something new and unexpected are improvisational conditions. Only improv is free enough to let something special, something unanticipated, something that changes things, happen. That is the nature of the spontaneous—and improvisation is the agent of spontaneity. Nothing else can open the door to the unexpected as improv can.

The Energy of Improvisation

The third great characteristic of improvisation is its sheer, flat-out energy. For Spolin, the words *energy* and *inspiration* are closely related. As she puts it, "inspiration in the theatre situation can best be described as energy."[7] There are numerous ways to understand this; but every performer knows that to be successful onstage requires not just hard work—that is a given; but also it requires an expenditure of all of the concentration and emotion that one has built up through intense preparation. When the actor, the speaker, or preacher is inspired, when what is said arises from a fire within, an energy in communication, whether as performance or public speech, is always the result.

Energy is not a matter of being frenetic, of jumping around or acting in a hyperanxious fashion. Energy expresses itself through passion. In Spolin's remarkable words, "People who are inspired may pace the floor or talk animatedly. Eyes sparkle, ideas pour forth, and the body releases its holds. If many people are inspired simultaneously, then the very air around them seems to sparkle and dance with excitement."[8] It cannot be better said. The preacher must so believe in what he or she is doing on the platform, must have so internalized it all, that it must generate an intensity and an excitement, a passion, in the overt, energetic expression of it. Even when the speaking is very quiet, as sometimes it must be, there will be an energy, an intensity, a controlled fire burning within it.

The speaker, the preacher, creates an energy field; and that energy field will be as large as he or she makes it. It is aided, of course, by microphone and in some cases the big screen; being seen and heard well are important to the reach of the energy field. But neither camera nor mike can *create* the energy field. Only the performer, the speaker—the preacher—can do that; and there is always a correlation between the degree of the preacher's passion for what is being communicated and the energy that is given off and spread throughout the hall. The principle is that energy creates energy, inspiration creates inspiration. It is virtually unfailing: If the preacher is inspired and energized, and turns loose to speak in such a way from the platform, that inspiration and energy, along with words and ideas and insights, will be transmitted and picked up by those who are in the room. It is also true that the inspiration and energy that is picked up by those present will never be greater or higher than what is conveyed by the speaker or preacher. For a preacher to become fully conscious of this precious reality is, in many cases, to change entirely the nature of how one preaches.

The Monological Dialogue of Improvisation

Improvisation's other momentous characteristic can only be expressed with a paradox—the sermon is a monologue, spoken by one person; in its character, style, and ultimate power, however, it actually turns into a dialogue of minds and hearts. Ironically, in African American worship forms, the call-and-response preaching model turns this monological dialogue into something resembling an overt dialogue: the preacher says something, and the congregation in unison repeats something back to the preacher, the preacher speaks again, and the congregation loudly responds together, and so on. In most non-African American congregations, however, this is not the pattern. The preacher alone does the speaking, with the congregation appearing to be passive and extremely quiet throughout.

However, the individuals who are there in worship are never passive, as all of us know from the times we have sat and listened to someone speak or preach. From the outside we appear to be just, well, listening; and yet we know that, depending on what is being said, we may be there or not. While we smile in the preacher's direction, we may be planning in our heads the afternoon's activities, or trying to solve a problem for tomorrow morning. When we are able to do that, it means that the preacher has captured no interest whatsoever from us—or, to be honest, is failing miserably.

We also know from our own experiences that when the preacher is talking about something that is, indeed, of interest to us, in our heads (while we smile or try to look pleasant) we are either arguing furiously with what is being said to us, or we are jumping up and down, mentally, at the sheer depth of our agreement. Our internal conversation is going full blast. As we sit and "listen," we are actually having a conversation in our own heads with the preacher. We are "replying" to what he or she is saying. We are agreeing or disagreeing; and in carrying on this conversation with the preacher—who has clearly engaged us to the point where we can focus on nothing but what is going on here and now—we are also carrying on a conversation with ourselves. It is a remarkable human ability.

The point is that this sermon we are listening to is no monologue—not at all. It is, or it can be, if we find it so dull and uninteresting as to have checked out to thoughts more important or interesting to us. Yet if the preacher is engaging us, if what we are hearing grabs and holds us, then—in our heads, and bodies, and imaginations—we are engaged in a full-scale, if silent, dialogue with every word and every sentence we are hearing. This is what a dialogical monologue is; it is, as it should be, the goal of every performer, as well as every one who speaks or preaches.

Not surprisingly, the preacher, by watching and listening keenly at the same time he or she is preaching, can all but "read" this dialogue taking place. The preacher, by watching closely while talking, can actually tell who is agreeing or disagreeing with what is being said; more than that, the preacher can usually tell if what is being said is creating a problem for a person here or there within the congregation. Nothing has to be said, since body language, facial expression, and even shifts in attention can signal to the preacher a particular attitude toward the words and ideas of the sermon. This, too, is a key part of the monological dialogue, since it provides the improvisational preacher with significant feedback that can, in turn, be folded into the sermon's very progress.

That Thing Called Charisma

In preparing to discuss the art of public speaking—and setting the bar high, which contemporary worship calls for—one thing must be recognized up front about those who set out to do it. Like all dramatic arts, powerful public speaking requires a combination of what social psychologists have long recognized as charisma and the learning and practice of specific speaking skills.

Charisma is that indefinable quality of personality that causes one to notice, or pay attention, to another person. It is not something that can be acquired or learned, not something conferred or worked for. It is a quality, instead, that demonstrates itself in an ability to attract attention, and, usually with that attention, followers. As such, it is a quality of leadership that sometimes results in an ability to win votes, or celebrity, or disciples. What is particularly striking about it, however, is that countless people may be said to possess some level of charisma.

There is no measure, however, by which one person may be said to have it while another does not. In one's own informal circle of friends, one or two people may emerge as the leaders of the group, respected and even followed by the others—and at that level one may be said to have a certain charismatic power. One may be a good teacher in a classroom, becoming not only teacher to his or her students, but a leader to whom the students are powerfully drawn; the teacher may be said to possess, in addition to teaching skills, charisma.

We can, and should, go so far as to say that *everyone* possesses, in some areas and amounts, some charisma, some personal attraction that is noticed by others, however small their number may be. Ironically, those who teach college courses in public speaking can most attest to the truth of this statement. In my speech teaching experience, I am always struck at the degree to which even the most unlikely person, *when placed in front of people with a subject that is dear to him or her,* evinces a noticeable charismatic attraction.

Two points need to be made here. First, if everyone has at least some charisma within them, as I believe they have, then everyone, potentially, has an ability to speak at least in a significantly compelling way in front of people. Clearly for that charisma to rise to the surface it must be connected to a *particular topic* that is held passionately and knowingly by the speaker; but when that topic is articulated publicly, it often belies a charismatic streak of personality. Second, the public speech forum—the lure of the stage, as it were—most often appeals to those whose charisma is somewhat higher than average, if we may say it that way. Great preachers, or speakers, are always powerfully charismatic figures; really good preachers are also possessors of significant charisma; and virtually all of those who aspire to be public speakers, in church, business, education, or wherever, are driven by a clear amount of charisma, a desire to stand before people as a leader.

Charisma alone, however, does *not* a great public speaker make. Great public speaking also requires a mastery of fundamentals, as well as a lifetime of practicing and polishing the basic, indispensable skills of public address. There are the rules of public speaking, readily available in any Introduction to Public Speaking course. They have to do with preparation and posture, earnestness and eye contact, speech development and diction, and a thousand other things. There must be the constant practice of speaking in front of people, giving speeches and then staying open to the feedback of those who hear. In these pages, too, we explore important elements involved in public speech—most of them not a reiteration of speech fundamentals, since it is hoped that those reading this will already know the basics.

So, there is a way, one that grows out of our common human life and interaction, to speak to large numbers of people—to preach—so that people are, every time they gather to hear the message preached, profoundly touched and moved by an experience of God and the things of God. We will call this *improvisational preaching*. There are ways to do it and ways not to, things that work and things that do not, rules and processes to be learned, practiced, and mastered. Anyone, young or old, whether experienced in public speaking or not, can do it.

Like any other skill, it only comes with work. It is important to remember as we begin that improvisational preaching is much more than just dramatic public speaking; it is communication of the very highest order. But it is even more than that, since at its very heart preaching delivers the Word of God. What we turn to in our remaining chapters is how to bring that Word of God most fully and deeply to life in any contemporary worship service.

Notes

1. John S. McClure, Ronald J. Allen, Dale P. Andrews, L. Susan Bond, Dan P. Moseley, and G. Lee Ramsey Jr., *Listening to Listeners: Homiletical Case Studies* (St. Louis: Chalice Press, 2004), 23.

2. Ibid., 59.

3. Viola Spolin, *Improvisation for the Theatre* (Evanston: Northwestern University Press, 1999), 14.

4. Ibid.

5. Stephen Nachmanovitch, *Free Play: Improvisation in Life and Art* (New York: Penguin Putnam, 1990), 23.

6. *Improvisation for the Theatre*, 4.

7. Ibid., 309.

8. Ibid.

CHAPTER TWO

THE RULES OF IMPROVISATIONAL PREACHING

L earn the rules and follow them: that is where all great improvisation begins, whether in music, in painting, or in any of the other creative arts—including both theatre and, in our case, public speaking or preaching. Improvisation, by its nature, is never totally impromptu; in fact, it cannot be. When it turns into that, it becomes unfocused, unmanageable, and ultimately uninteresting; it shows itself as both confused and confusing.

When the rules of a particular form of improvisation are learned and followed, however, the invariable result is that a very good performance is turned into a great, and an often memorable, one. We would not be entirely honest if, as preachers, we did not acknowledge that we wish to create and deliver the kinds of sermons that will, with God's leading and blessing, not just be memorable but will change the lives of people in our worship experiences.

In this chapter, we examine the rules that guide improvisational preaching. In principle, they are no different than the rules that guide the composer or performer of improvisational art, music, or theatre. Ironically, they sound different since we are simply not used to seeing them articulated for and applied to public address, particularly the kind that goes on in today's new forms of Christian worship.

Two points need to be kept in mind. First, the rules are essential for improvisational speaking. These are not rules for beginners, to be left behind when one feels experienced or able to fly on one's own. They *are* for beginners at public speaking, and preaching, of course; but as any improvisational musician would say, the rules are the fundamentals, and no matter how good one gets, or how much sophistication one's work achieves, the fundamentals are always there, undergirding everything. If they are forgotten or ignored, the finished product tends to fall apart. At certain levels of experience, to be sure, rules (as they say) are made to be broken, but even then the great musician is always aware of the presence and importance of the rule when and if it is deliberately broken.

The second point to remember is that the rules are not only designed to constrain what one does—that is, to keep the perform-ance under control and on track—but also the rules exist, literally, to set the performance *fully free*. The rules provide the fundamen-tal platform for taking off to achieve the greatest possible heights of both creativity and experiential excitement in what one does. Ironically, not to follow the rules is to become less than what one might otherwise be in the work that one does.

What, then, are the rules of improvisational public speaking, i.e., contemporary preaching? In this chapter we shall discuss eight such rules.

Master the Fundamentals of Speaking

First, the improvisational contemporary preacher must master the basics of public speaking—everything begins there. At first, this sounds like it should go without saying, (as, strangely, do many of the rules of improvisation, though that is one of the most deceptive dimensions of all improvisation itself). It is too often assumed, particularly by young preachers, that there are real sermons, meaning well-prepared, carefully crafted sermons; and then there are improvised sermons, or those sermons to be preached when one has not been left with too much preparation time this week. Few things, however, are more destructive to good, or even great, improvisational preaching than this dichotomy.

Granted, much of what we can call the preparation for improvisational speech is not of a "this week" kind; it is the preparation that is rooted in years of work, study, and practice. One does not study the history of improvisational jazz music, for example (of whatever kind), without discovering that it always arises from years of preparation. The improvisational musician learns musical scales, for example, that tough, often boring process of drilling and drilling, practicing and practicing. Those scales, in all of their variations, then become the very foundation for everything that the jazz improvisational artist does. Chord progressions are founded on those scales; arpeggios are a way of playing the chords in progression, founded, again, on the learning of those scales. Melodies, too, arise from the scales and arpeggios, melodies that can, within the rules, be embellished and turned into new songs, or new riffs and movements of old songs.

To talk about improvisational preaching, or improv public speaking, is to assume a significant amount of past preparation. There are "scales" to be learned, as it were, if we take the scale as a metaphor for learning the basics, the fundamentals of an art form—which public address is every bit as much as public musical performance. In this case, though, we are assuming that one knows or has even mastered the art of public speaking. Has one had, for example, a good speech class at the higher educational level? Does one know how to develop and deliver a speech in front of people—following all of the basic rules of what good public speaking is?

The rules that govern public speaking itself have to be understood, not just in the head, but in practice—rules concerning such things as posture, movement, gesturing, eye contact, and the use of one's voice with variety and pacing and proper modulation. There are basic prepreparation rules that govern how speeches are devised and put together, rules concerning one central idea per speech, the rules for good organization and outlining, as well as the rules about beginnings and endings of speeches. These are the "scales" on which improvisational public speaking rest. This book is not about those basics—though a summary of them can be found in my book *Preaching Without Notes*, from Abingdon Press (2001); they can also be found in countless basic books about public speaking. But one has to have studied those books, or taken a good basic speech course or two in order to learn those fundamentals. That has to precede the process of learning to grow as an effective improvisational preacher.

Thoroughly Prepare Every Sermon

The second rule that underlies all memorable improvisational preaching is that what appears to be spontaneous and even off the cuff when spoken is always carefully and thoroughly prepared in advance. The rule, in fact, can be extended to say that the better the improvisational sermon is—the more memorable it is—the more time and effort has gone into its advance preparation.

When one comes to the task of improvisational preaching with a mastery of the public speaking scales, then this rule kicks in: prepare thoroughly, not in that larger sense of knowing the basics, but in the sense of preparing this sermon, the one to be delivered this week. In short, improvisational preaching is never off the top of the head. It may draw on things that have been stored away, and that may end up being part of its spontaneity, but one should never count on that happening.

The improvised sermon is the well-prepared sermon. It is worked out in all of its details in advance of preaching. Biblical texts are studied carefully and exegetical notes are compiled; a central idea is winnowed out and the hundred other ideas that might be possible are laid aside for another time and another sermon. An outline, whether in a classic form or in a more contemporary sequential style (see chapter 5 here or my book *Preaching Without Notes*), is devised. Materials to be used with the sermon, whether illustrations, stories, or video clips, are carefully planned. Nothing, in a sense, is left to chance. That process provides the groundwork for the best possible improvisational sermon to be preached.

It should be clear by now that there are two kinds of improvisational sermons—the well-prepared ones and the ill-prepared, or even unprepared, ones. Strange as it may seem, savvy listeners in contemporary services can invariably tell the difference. Or, more accurately, they can tell when an improvised sermon has not been well prepared in advance, and it is never a happy awareness. There is no substitute for good sermon preparation—even though the sermon will be actually preached in a strikingly different way than most traditional sermons have been for the past few decades.

Create Interaction in Your Speaking

The third rule of improvisational preaching is that one speak in a way that is consciously interactive with those who share the speaking. This is the genius of improv in virtually all of its forms. Another way of saying this is that in preaching one does not try to control everything; the trick is to know that anything can happen, and that applies to the preacher's own internal life during the speaking itself or to the setting's external life, which means that something can go on with any person present at any time. Everything has to be taken as it comes and assimilated into the preacher's ongoing sermon.

This is possible, however, only after the planning has been thorough and meticulous. The preacher prepares carefully what he or she is going to say. The main point and the outline are carefully crafted. The sense of how it will be presented is fully thought through. There is no substitute for well-grounded preparation so that, in a sense, nothing is left to chance. All of this, moreover, has been done fully bathed in prayer.

When this is done, the dominate process of improvisational speaking is spontaneous interaction, energized by a sense of openness with everyone. The best way to describe this is to call what happens an *emergent sermon*. Even though it is well prepared, everything the preacher says will be rethought or thought through anew during the ongoing act of speaking. It is this thinking freshly, thinking on one's feet, that ultimately lies at the heart of turning a monological one-sided event into a dialogical, interactive event.

Here is where the great power of improvisational public speaking lies: in its ability to be so interactive and unexpected that congregants are mesmerized—but in a fully conscious, completely engaged way—mentally, emotionally, and even spiritually.

There are essentially two underlying elements of this dimension of public address. The first is that, in a public gathering, literally, very literally, anything *can* happen; and the preacher needs to be constantly on the lookout, during the sermon itself, for out-of-the-ordinary things. The public speaking instructions go something like this: While you talk, be constantly watching as your eyes (with good eye movement) take in the entire congregation. Be sure to listen to and look at what is going on within the congregation; preachers can be very surprised sometimes at the visual or even audible signals that are sent from various places within the worship space. While you speak, make rhetorical questions a part of your improvisational presentation; and while you do not actually expect visual or verbal responses to your rhetorical question, invariably there are some, and picking up on them can often become a very important part of the interactional nature of the sermon itself.

Make rhetorical statements that, in a sense, seek affirmations about what you are saying; such statements are usually simple and direct, asking for a deliberately returned nod of the head as an involved, if subtle, response. All of this is seen, in its most overt fashion, in the call-and-response process that plays such a large part in African American preaching. It can, and should, though, also find its way into contemporary preaching as well, though the responses will tend to be smaller and less obvious.

The second dimension concerns the need of the preacher to keenly understand that when the sermon is open-ended, spontaneous, and improvisationally delivered, people who sit quietly and smile while listening are *never* sitting passively and unthinkingly. The "iceberg" effect is always taking place. As the preacher speaks, inside the head of every listener a complex churning of language, ideas, and emotions is going on, as it does for all of us most of the time.

So it is at church, too. The task of a good improvisational sermon is to be so compelling that it can actually interrupt the internal conversation that everyone brings into worship with them, causing the words of the sermon to become the *subject* of that highly active, internal, albeit silent, conversation-with-self in which every congregant is engaged. The point is that the preacher must remember that what appears to be an active speaker and a collection of passive congregants is nothing of the sort; and to think such a thing, or even assume it, is to make a serious mistake. Even when congregants were singing and dancing a few minutes before, overtly involved, but now have settled quietly in their seats to listen—they have not gone from active to passive; they have gone from *externally active* to *internally active*, and to mistake that is to miss the profound dynamic of effective, improvisational public speaking.

We all need periodically to be reminded as well that no two individuals ever respond in the same way to even the same words we speak; that words, for all of us, often have deep and complex "biographies" in each of our lives. If the preacher, for example, uses the word *father*—making clear that he or she is not talking about God, but about a human father, that word itself can immediately set off a complex host of cognitive meanings and, probably more important, emotionally charged, vividly sketched meanings and images from almost everyone's past. What may mean one thing, of low emotional value to the preacher, may and often will set off an entirely different set of emotional responses for this person or that one in the congregation.

The congregant will *react*, however he or she looks sitting in a seat, to whatever is set off in his or her head, rather than to the preacher's use of that word. That is the principle on which all communication, even the communication of public speaking, is built. Obviously, the extension of that principle would mean that if there are two hundred people all of whom hear the preacher refer to one's father, there would most likely be two hundred different responses to that word, some of which could be quite extreme. The question is whether the preacher who uses that word would be sensitive enough in both watching and listening to the congregation to actually pick up where the most extreme responses to the word might be experienced. In improvisational preaching, everything that the preacher says is reacted to, and even acted upon, by everyone who is present; that is the nature of the *interactive dynamic*, the monological dialogue of the speaking. It is the preacher's responsibility to stay both spontaneous and keenly aware of every response and bit of feedback that comes to him or her from those who only appear to be passively listening.

Hold Emotions Back—Let Energy Out

The fourth rule of improvisational preaching has to do with the preacher's emotions and energies; we may state the rule as "keep *emotions* in check but turn your *energies* loose."

Emotions in public speaking, even in an improvisational setting, are always something of a problem. Not that they should be withheld, since when we deal with emotional matters, it is expected that our emotions must show. There is no question, moreover, but that we should be authentic in our emotional expressions, even in front of people. Onstage, in fact, we expect emotion. Public speaking on issues of profound importance cannot help but conjure up emotions, even, or particularly, for the speaker. Indeed, we are always suspect when we talk about emotional issues, particularly of a personal nature, and yet we appear to be suspiciously unemotional. When that happens, something is clearly out of whack as far as the hearer or worshipper is concerned.

Still, the rule is that it is never appropriate to go over the edge emotionally when speaking to people. Emotions, that is, must not be curtailed, but must be *held in check*. No tears in the pulpit—that may be the most explicit way to say it. This is not because we pretend that we are somehow above tears; in fact, we need for people to know that tears are often an inevitable part of life; and that preachers are not immune to them. And, as many will point out, the deepest possible emotions, often accompanied by intense tears, are often a part of the dramatic productions that we attend, the classic plays from Shakespeare to Molière to Tennessee Williams. We are used to tears onstage. Those are the cases, though, that come to the viewer only indirectly, since that fourth wall about which we spoke earlier is always in place. We are watching something through a glass in a sense, or from a distance. We are protected, in a very real way, from those tears.

We need to emphasize, though, that in the sermon preached improvisationally the protection between performer and audience, that invisible fourth wall, is gone. The contact we expect and need is *direct*, not indirect; and when this happens, for us to confront a depth of emotion that can prompt tears places the hearers or audience or congregation in an odd position. We are observers of tears who are somehow expected to participate in the tears, since that participation is expected of us throughout the interaction of the communicative sermon itself. But when the preacher is reduced to tears, the congregants do not know what to do. Congregants are put in what can only be described as an embarrassing situation. They may empathize with the preacher, and may even share the preacher's pain, but they are seldom moved to tears themselves; and in not being moved to share the tears the situation that results is, at best, an awkward one. Showing emotion, but holding back from going over the edge becomes the best directive for the improvisational sermon.

The other side of that coin, however, has to do with the expenditure of *energy* in the improv sermon. This is a subject to which Viola Spolin, the great improvisational teacher, devoted considerable attention. Energy equals animation, or a sense of sheer emotional *intensity* that translates into the complete involvement of the performer, the preacher, in what he or she is doing and saying. It is to be completely consumed by the task, the subject, the goal at hand. It is not nonchalant. It is not blasé. It is not matter-of-fact. It is the reflection of a belief that what one is doing at this moment in time is the most important thing in the entire world; that one would rather be doing this, on this subject, with you people, more than anything else that one could even contemplate doing.

One cannot in this process, as Spolin says, show any sign of tiredness or boredom; one cannot, that is, *not* be intensely driven in the pursuit of this speaking task. In her often understated way, she writes at one point, "an actor without energy is worthless."[1] Following this rule, we could undoubtedly say that a preacher without energy is, well, not worth very much either.

Energy, in this sense, does not mean being frenetic. It does not mean that one races about on the platform or stage, that one is constantly jumping about or waving arms. It does not mean that one prowls the stage, always ready to pounce in some way or other. Energy in this sense actually refers to more than the intensity we talked about earlier. It can often be quiet, and sometimes even silent and still; and, in fact, it needs to be from time to time. It certainly does not mean shouting or seeing how rapidly one can talk;

both of those are invariably distracting or even annoying. Those are not signs of energy as much as they are signs of nervousness and being out of control in front of people. To be energized, however, is to be fully and unabashedly centered or focused on what one is saying, on how one is saying it, and, most important, on the people with whom one is speaking. It is to be thoroughly *concentrated* on the task at hand—not just on the words that one is speaking, but on the full range of the situation within this space. It is not to be so serious that one cannot laugh, or lead others in the joy of laughter; but it is to be fully coiled, so concentrated on the work of this moment that every congregant is actually pulled, without reservation, into this moment as well. That is what every stage actor must accomplish, and it is only with the expenditure of internal energy that this ultimately can be done. It is also what the improvisational preacher must accomplish as well—which is why the improvisational preacher must be unrelenting in maintaining the highest concentrated energy possible within the preaching event.

Create and Resolve Suspense

The fifth rule for improvisational preaching is that in speaking one must create and resolve classic dramatic suspense. This involves the creation of a problem of some sort, often an important one—a problem that is both alive and relevant to those who take part in the worship experience. From the problem to the solution, from the dilemma to the outcome, from a sense of depression, failure, or loss to a sense of joy, hope, and victory—it is the classic dramatic model. It is also the gospel message of Christ Jesus. But it works the best when it takes practical form and is set up in a suspenseful way. It is the suspense of *not knowing how something will, in the end, be overcome or resolved.*

Since one of the underlying motivations of improvisation itself is unpredictability and unexpectedness, the sermon must be filled with tensions—tensions that produce suspense, but that, in the end, resolve themselves in a way that gives both release and pleasure. That is what we expect from a great play or film, or even from a great musical performance; as odd as it may sound, it is also what we have a right to expect from a great sermon.

We need, though, to be clear about what is involved in this; and the idea (again) of jazz improvisation provides the useful metaphor. The entire piece of jazz music has to be unified; it is a whole, well written and completely planned in advance. But to one who is listening, that overall unity is often *disguised* or *withheld* until a given point where it all begins to come together, to make sense; there is that point at which the unity finally starts to become visible. There is, in all such improvisational music, always a tension between its unity and its seeming disunity; or at least, in the playing, the musician wants the audience not to know until the appropriate moment how it is all going to work out. The musician knows, but wants to hold the listener in suspense, often for just as long as possible.

The parallel to the improvisational sermon is not difficult to see, and, not surprisingly, a great power of the improv sermon is this tension between the unity of the whole and the speaker's desire to withhold a full view of that unity for as long as possible. This, in itself, is done in the planning of the sermon, of course. One sets up a group of ideas—I have in other places called them *sequences*— that are explained one by one; the preacher knows how they will all come together, but the hearer does not immediately know, so must both puzzle over the ideas, and enjoy, on faith, that they will come to a useful, even an important, resolution. *Where is this going?* is exactly what the improvisational musician wants the hearer to puzzle over; it is what a film director like Alfred Hitchcock wants the viewer to ask during the opening hour of a movie with its pieces strung together in what appears to be a haphazard, unrelated fashion. The tension clearly rises the farther the tune or movie goes along—and then the resolution, at some point, begins to emerge. It is the way of a very good improvisational sermon as well.

In such a sermon, there are numerous smaller tensions, no less important to the overall performance than the larger one. In jazz music, for example, the tensions, both large and small, are built into the music; and it is the tensions, along with their resolutions that keep everything interesting and unexpected. Just when an improvisational musician believes the audience has everything figured out, an unplanned movement, a riff on an unexpected chord, the shifting of the key, or some other change is introduced to keep things off-balance until that movement when the final resolution is to come to pass.

With practice, the improvisational preacher will become every bit as good as the improv jazz performer in working with tensions to hold, and increase, the congregation's full participation in and enjoyment of the sermon. The preacher has to begin, though, by understanding the sermon as a whole, as a structure that can, in a real sense, be *diagrammed* as a picture. It will have its low, slow sections—high in intensity, of course, but with a deliberateness designed, perhaps, to soothe; and then it will hit an unexpected chord that will shift its direction, moving to a different mood.

There will be the crescendos and decrescendos in the sermon, movements of building up and coming down; it will have its unexpected, even strikingly spontaneous statements, its planned and carefully constructed arguments, and then its asides—and often the asides will carry the preacher's most important words. The sermon will have its own accents, its points of pause, even silence, and those places at which the words will have to rush by at a fever pitch. There will be times to hold one's hands perfectly still at one's side, and times to use both hands and arms to be as boldly assertive as one can. Some sermons will establish wonderfully repetitive melodies, sweet, even soothing lines; and then, in the midst of those memorable (and planned) phrases will come unexpected, even jarring words. This is the nature of improvisation, whether of painting, of moviemaking, or music—or of public speaking. The tensions are in the variations, and the variations will, themselves, stand at the heart of the power—and constant unexpectedness—of improvisational preaching.

Communicate, Don't Perform

The sixth important rule of improvisational public speaking is that the speaker should always—always—concentrate on communication and not on performance. In a sense, this seems to run somewhat counter to the whole emphasis on preaching as theatre, or, specifically, with preaching as improvisational theatre or performance. But in using such a metaphor for this process, we are concentrating primarily on style or on approach. We are not trying to avoid the idea that in improvisational speech there is a strong element of performance; there clearly is. One is onstage, often (or even usually) quite literally. In most contemporary worship settings, the old pulpit is gone. It tended to hold the preacher in, again sometimes quite literally. For the most part, it has now been replaced with an open platform, a stage. On it, at most, will be a small podium, if the preacher needs a place to post his or her notes; or something resembling a desk, sometimes literally a low desk on which one may set a page of notes, or even some objects or props for the work.

Most often, though, the stage is open, bare. The preacher is free to move about; and what must be practiced and learned is stage movement. That means having a central spot that is home in a sense, a place to stand and from which to speak; it will also be the place from which various stage movements will start and to which they will return. As a result, appearance becomes very important, even though the actual form of dress for preaching will depend entirely on the requirements of the setting and the church's tradition or mode of being. It usually takes time, practice, and even experience for the preacher in such a setting to become comfortable onstage. Self-consciousness will never go away entirely, and may, for some, reemerge at the beginning of virtually every sermon. After some practice, however, it will be minimized; and after one is three or four sentences into the sermon, if one has planned carefully, the self-consciousness will evaporate completely.

The key question concerning the performance dimension of the sermon usually revolves around how dramatic one should be with the sermon. Anyone who has grown up on a high school or even a college stage (as numerous preachers have) knows that there is a kind of performance language. There are ways to be dramatic. What needs to be kept always in mind, however, is that preaching is *not* acting. And the very real danger in comparing preaching to theatre or the stage at all is that it conjures up for many people the harsh realities—not of acting, but of *overacting*. Overacting is always bad acting. It calls attention to itself; it even represents an unintended parody of acting.

So the answer to the question of *How dramatic should the sermon, even the improvised sermon, be?* is that it should *not be dramatic at all*, despite the relationship between improvisation and the dramatic arts. That is the only way to prevent the biggest potential problem of the amateur stage from occurring on the preaching platform. When the sermon is overly dramatic, or overacted, the sermon is, for all practical purposes, ruined. The artifices of acting, those mannerisms, movements, gestures, and vocal intonations do nothing but call attention to themselves, often with humorous overtones, and the thrust of even a well-prepared sermon is lost.

So, while there are obvious connections between the idea of performance and the sermon, particularly when we discuss it in the context of theatrical improvisation, the sermon must not be performed. The dangers of performance, or even the dangers in trying to conjure up the mechanics of stage performance, are simply too great.

The solution, instead, arises from this requirement: that the preacher must focus all understandings and energies on the process of *communication* rather than performance. At one level, this sounds like a cliché, but it truly is not; or at least it need not be. Spolin, in teaching improvisational theatre, even called attention to this distinction in her training of actors. She called the dangers of overacting a kind of exhibitionism, noting that such "exhibitionism withers away when the student-actor begins to see members of the audience not as judges or censors . . . but as a group with whom he [or she] is sharing an experience."[2]

The point is simple and straightforward. Actors, even improvisational actors, invariably perform in order to receive a judgment from the audience, usually an approval of a job well done, a play well performed or a very entertaining evening. Spolin wanted even her improvisational performers to see what they did *in a different way*; that what they did was engage in an *interactive form of communication*, one that fully engaged the audience, and did so in a manner that carried no artifice whatsoever from the stage itself. In a sense, her argument holds for virtually all those who perform improvisationally: the desire is to *communicate*, whether it is with one's music, one's art or idea or set of ideas, as in stage work; strangely enough, anyone who pays close attention to even improvisational comics knows that virtually all of them—granted there are exceptions—find their comedy in something they really want to say.

So while the contemporary preacher is, in part, performer, the preacher needs to understand his or her role solely in terms of communication—one person reaching, or reaching out to, many. The fourth wall, as we said earlier—that wall which, in classic theatre, separates the actor from the audience, is gone. It doesn't exist in this setting, and the speaker's role—the improvisational preacher's task—is to reach and hold those who watch and hear the preacher and the words.

If the preacher, though, is not to act onstage, but, instead, to communicate from the stage, then what sense of identity should the preacher take on in order to facilitate the process of communication? The answer is that the preacher, we might say, is to speak naturally. One is to be fully oneself, to talk in one's regular voice, to make normal movements and gestures—inasmuch as possible, literally to plan nothing. With today's microphones, the talking need not even be louder than one would talk with a friend on a walk through the park. It will, of course, be animated talk, filled with expressiveness—precisely the kind of talk in which one engages around a dinner table with a set of good, lively friends. To think about what this kind of talk is like is to get a good idea of what the sermon needs to sound like. Both the talk and the movements will have periods of ease and periods of intensity, periods of deliberateness and periods of high certainty, but all of those things are normal in our dealings with each other as well.

What those who have studied acting (as opposed to those who have only acted when called upon) will recognize, however, is that what we are describing represents the highest ideal of the professional actor. Even though the stage or screen actor is dealing with scripted lines meticulously committed to memory, the task of the professional is to speak the lines in as normal a manner as possible; and those who can do that have, indeed, mastered their stage or screen craft. They speak learned lines as though they were speaking them for the first time, making them sound like fully and completely improvised or spontaneous conversational language around a dining room table. Every line that a great actor like Gene Hackman says on the screen sounds utterly and absolutely natural or normal, like he is making it up on the spot as he speaks.

It is that illusion by the professional actor that the improvisational preacher is to achieve naturally in preaching the sermon. The lines are neither scripted nor learned; the ideas and the general form for speaking are both prepared and learned, however. But when the moment of speaking arrives, the words are spoken naturally, as naturally as a Gene Hackman would say them had they been put in his mouth.

Provide No Distractions to Speaking

We all understand that in our digitalized culture, we have entered the era of PowerPoint and video—with everything imaginable projected via computer onto the large screens in most of today's worship spaces. Nor is there any way that we cannot, or will not, utilize these marvelous new electronic devices in our worship services. We will use a wide range of images from nature, placed over music, as a way to give visual content to our preservice activities. We will project the lyrics to the worship songs and choruses that we sing together. At various places in worship, we will enhance liturgical activity by projecting images and moving pictures of religious realism and symbolism. We will greet visitors with live images of them from wherever they happen to be seated. Over the Scripture reading, or some aspect of storytelling, we will play a video clip from a movie. Aside from the new forms of music that resound through our sanctuaries and spaces, the one thing that lets people know that something new and exciting is going on here is the constancy of the video screens that provide a subtext to our entire contemporary worship experience.

Something must be said here, however, about the unique and essential role of the new sermon in this worship experience. It is that the preacher and his or her words and movements must take center stage for the presentation of the message from God's Word; moreover, everything we are talking about in this book is designed to prepare the preacher to generate the excitement and power in that spoken presentation to equal anything that, up to that point, has appeared on those overhead screens. By and large, preachers are notorious for their lack of confidence in their speaking, particularly when they are just starting out, or when they are trying new things in their sermon presentations. As a result, most are only too happy to think that something on the big screen might help to "lift" or "add zest" to their prepared sermon.

If I think I need help, many think, *look what has finally come to my aid. I will put my whole sermon outline on PowerPoint and do that unfolding point by point on the screen, and, to really give what I am saying some juice, I will start out with a film clip for three minutes, and then intersperse my sermon with three or four other short clips, ending with the ending of this film or that.* While we are not about to suggest that there is something inherently wrong with outlines and film clips on a big screen, what we have just gone through is a recipe for how to kill a good sermon. So the rule for effective, potent improvisational preaching can be simply stated: don't do anything with visuals, music, or PowerPoint that will detract from the power of the voice, presence, or personality of the preacher who is speaking, in an exciting fashion, the Word of God.

There is no formula, of course, for when to use the screens and when not to, as far as the sermon is concerned. But when the preacher is at his or her best, with a well-prepared and exciting improvisational sermon, the worst thing that the worship planners can do is to awkwardly shift attention from the preacher to one of the big overhead screens. If a video clip is wanted, start the sermon with it, and use it then as a take-off point for what the preacher has prepared to say. When the preacher is speaking, and speaking well—meaning that the people are intently focused on the preacher's improvisational work—the worst thing that can happen is for that to be interrupted by something flashing overhead. There might, on rare occasions, be illustrations that take the form of a short video clip, but they should be few and far between, and be so well selected and set up that they will continue the flow of the preacher's words, rather than come as a disjuncture to the movement and focus of the preacher's work. Be particularly cautious, moreover, about ending a sermon with a video clip, no matter how good—since the appeal of the sermon's end can seldom come more powerfully than from the mouth of the messenger.

As to PowerPoint, the argument for its use throughout the sermon is that it allows the main points of the preacher's sermon to be visually hooked into people's minds, as well as just entering through their ears. When the preacher's outline is projected on the screen, along with printed Scripture that will be read here and there through the sermon, it is somehow believed that people will remember it all better, or will have an easier time writing down notes on the sermon to take with them when they leave.

It is a strange view, or argument, particularly when it comes from contemporary worship leaders who worry about whether worshippers will have a genuine experience of God when they gather. The preacher whose sermon outline is projected, or unfurled item by item on the overhead screen, simply does not have a chance of speaking in a way that will create an experience or leave a lasting impression. There may be some admiration at the elegance of the numerous outlines above the preacher's head, or even some gratitude that one can carry away a few written notes; but as far as people being moved by the sermon, nothing is deadlier to that than having attention diverted from the preacher to the overhead screen.

Preach Always without Notes

The eighth and final rule of improvisational preaching has to do with memory: it is that the contemporary preacher must learn to trust his or her memory and take time to memorize the sermon notes.

First there is the matter of trusting one's memory, a subject that I discussed at length in my book *Preaching Without Notes*. The human memory, as the ancient Greeks understood very well, is a remarkable human facility, a product of that miraculous organ called the brain. We are seldom taught or even encouraged to memorize anything, except when confronted with a school examination of one sort or another when we were young. What great professional speakers know is that few things make for more potent public speaking than the use of memory. Ironically, it is the one mental skill by which professional actors and actresses *live*; whether for stage or screen, they become very good at memorizing, verbatim, enormous blocks of material, their dialogue. For them, the use of the memory becomes second nature.

The effective improvisational preacher is not afraid of memorizing. In fact, the effective preacher knows that one of the true keys to unlocking new joy and genuine creativity in the contemporary preaching ministry lies in getting rid of all the scripts—including the sermon script—and becoming as good as one can be at memorizing. Despite the low use of memory, the twentieth century has seen an explosion of research in the area of human memory, most of it tied to special problems in learning and education. The questions about how learning and memory are connected to each other have driven psychological, sociological, neurological, and even hereditary research. How—and how well—are we able to remember things? While we now know, for example, that there are a number of different kinds of memory—long-term, short-term, working memory, visual memory, and so on—the one that particularly applies to public speaking is short-term memory. With it, we learn to quickly master for virtually perfect recall lists of ideas and concepts that form the basis for speech and sermon outlines. Moreover, from the preacher's perspective, we know that with short-term memory, what we have memorized quickly fades as well—which we need it to do after a given Sunday, so that the space can be clearer, so to speak, for memorizing next Sunday's sermon outline.

More important, we have learned that short-term memory is a practiced skill, like any other skill. The mind is a muscle, in a sense, that learns to do, and do well, what it is trained to do. This is true for anyone whose mind is in decent working order. The more that one commits things to short-term memory, the less time and effort it takes to actually memorize over time. Practice, in fact, makes perfect, or almost perfect. To say "I cannot memorize very well" is the same as saying "I cannot type very well." But you could if you practiced doing it: that is what the educators are telling us.

The bottom line is that improvisational speaking, and preaching, requires that it be done without notes. Despite how well prepared it must be, it must still come across to those who hear it and share it as someone just talking to us. Not preaching to us. Not lecturing to us. Not trying to get us to do this or that. It is someone who just stood in front of us and, with passion, shared his or her heart. No papers. No looking for something on the podium or table. Just speaking from the heart. That is the secret to improvisation. It is a heart-based form of public speaking—and humans everywhere, regardless of age or even culture, are without question drawn to it and invariably moved by it.

What we have called the rules for improvisational public speaking do, indeed, make the difference between an average public speaker, i.e., preacher in our case, and someone who wishes to rise above the average. They form the difference between someone who is good or competent, and someone who wishes, with practice, to rise to a select group of outstanding preachers. They form the difference in public speaking and preaching between an ordinary standard and one who truly wishes to reach for the gold standard. But our journey has only begun. Now we turn to the content of the improvisational sermon, a subject that will take us from the Bible into the expanding and essential world of story and storytelling.

Notes

1. Viola Spolin, *Improvisation for the Theatre* (Evanston: Northwestern University Press, 1999), 309.
2. Ibid., 13.

CHAPTER THREE

STORY: IMPROVISATION'S FUNDAMENTAL FORM

The highest form of improvisational speech today—whether in comedy, politics, education, or, for our purposes, in contemporary preaching—is the story. This is not just "the story," as in "I am going to tell you a story"; but it is the "story as model," the "story" as *fundamental paradigm* for what one plans to say. For more than a hundred years, in creating the increasingly complicated world of electronic media, our culture has come to live and die by stories and storytelling. Today's young people and young adults are actually "wired," as it were, for stories. This has been succinctly captured by Leonard Sweet, a theologian of popular culture, in his statement that "In the postmodern world, the future belongs to the 'storytellers.'"[1] He is right. It does.

To become an effective contemporary or improvisational preacher today is to learn the art of the story: what it is, how it works, how to devise it from the Bible as well as from human experience—and, just as importantly, how to tell it. No matter what one wishes to say, no matter what kind of message one wants to present, if it is to reach maximum effectiveness, it must be embodied in the form of a story. This is not a single way of doing things, however, not something that becomes monotonous because of repetition; in fact, one of the beauties of the story form is how many different incarnations it can take. Every story can actually be as exciting, and even as compelling, as the one before. Each one, in short, can be filled with surprise and discovery.

First, the improvisational preacher must learn to find, create, and tell stories. They are everywhere around us, so much so that we cannot live without them. They make us who and what we are. Our days are filled, for example, with "news *stories.*" Some news stories are short—a murder was committed, a gang robbed a store, a couple led police on a high-speed chase. Some are long, sometimes extending over days: a man holds a family hostage, an airliner is missing, an offensive in the war takes time. We follow the news as an unending string of "stories," all related, and yet not related at all. There are other kinds of stories as well—the stories of 60 *Minutes,* the longest running, top-rated show in history. There are "documentary" news stories, the "real story" of Bonnie and Clyde, complete with decades-old film clips; the "story" of American jazz or baseball and how they came to be. We *like* "real stories" of real people and events, told A&E Channel style, or History Channel style.

Then there are movies, endless movies, all great "stories," some of course better than others; but Americans alone spend millions of dollars every single week watching movies—to say nothing about the global movie audiences. Comic stories, nostalgic stories, love stories, horror stories, stories of crime and violence—we live by the movies and their stories. Movies are related to novels, often the ones from which the movies are made. The great novel writers of our time, writers like John Grisham, overflow with stories that sell by the millions.

Then there are television's stories—from situation comedies like *Friends* and *Everybody Loves Raymond* to the soap operas to the so-called reality shows, those shows that create wild escapades in which, presumably, the outcomes are never known "in advance." Even the thousands of daily television commercials are designed as mini stories, one-minute "dramas" designed to catch the eye and create a memorable moment.

Then there is that other "story" dimension of life, particularly among young people, but older ones, too—the "stories" embedded and embodied in video games. Games are no longer games; they are elaborate stories in which the game player or players not only become "characters" in the stories themselves; they also determine how the stories will be "played out," who will live, who will die, and who will do what to whom.

We do virtually nothing today without stories—to the point where they are actually invisible to us—like the "invisible" water fish swim in. Teachers at all levels of school know that if they wish to teach something of importance, something that will grab and hold attention, something that will be remembered and used, it must be told as a story. College professors of all disciplines know that lectures no longer work; they must be "stories," told well—and when they are told well, we are more than willing to listen and enjoy for long stretches of time. Stories *do* "hold us," no matter whether they come from a movie or TV show, from a stage play, from a video game, or even from an excellent storyteller standing in front of us.

What remains, it appears, is for preachers in contemporary settings to learn the same lesson. It is necessary to distinguish two things about the story and its relationship to improvisational preaching.

The first is that stories themselves become a staple of the sermon itself, stories that in spoken form take from three to five minutes. These are stories that are literally woven into the fabric of the sermon, breathing life and vitality into the sermon every step of its way. Here we are concerned with such questions as, *Where does one get stories for the sermon? How are stories for the sermon put together?*

and, *How does a story become more than just a story?* or, *If Jesus used stories as a basis for so much of his preaching, what did he use them for?* How, in short, does one find and use stories in the improvisational sermon?

The second large dimension of story that the improvisational preacher must work through concerns the process of creating the sermon itself "in the shape of a story." This goes beyond story making and storytelling, as important as those are for the sermon. It means realizing that *a story is not a sermon*, that telling a good story is not the same as preaching a sermon; and it means that *a sermon is not just a good story*. It is much more complicated than that. A sermon, however, for the improvisational, contemporary pulpit must be created "like a story," or in a story format. A documentary film, for example, is not a "story" as such—though it presents its "information," what it wishes to say, in the "form of a story." That's what the improvisational sermon must do as well—if it is to function at maximum efficiency, with top-drawer drawing, holding, and teaching power.

We begin with stories for sermons, starting at the beginning: What is a story?

A story is an account of an event of some kind that is told *in a dramatic fashion*. This means that it is developed and told in the sermon in a progressive form, built from beginning to end with the suspense of unexpectedness and outcome. Kenneth Burke, the literary philosopher, says that a story can be built with two kinds of suspense. The first is the suspense of not knowing how it will end—the suspense of surprise. It is building the story piece by piece, turning over first one thing and then another, without "giving away" the ending. It is the ending that we begin to anticipate and try to figure out, the ending that will hold the "surprise" for us in the story. It is the suspense of what will happen next as we move on toward the outcome.

The second is the suspense of *anticipation* itself. It is the suspense that can readily be aroused even when we know how something is going to end, the suspense we experience by participating fully in the "buildup" to that ending. As Burke describes it, this is the equivalent of watching someone gradually but steadily stretch a rubber band, knowing that, as it has before, it is going to snap in a mighty way, but still feeling the suspense as it is held taut before the snap actually comes. In the first, the suspense of surprise, we experience it the first time we see a movie, or hear a story; but in the second, we choose to see the same movie, or hear the same story, over and over again—and each time, it is a new kind of suspense in which we participate.

In improvisational preaching of the gospel, sometimes we do not know the outcome of a good biblical story, particularly if we are hearing it for the first time. Often, though, we do know the outcome, we know "how the story ends," so it becomes very much a matter of telling the "old story" in a highly suspenseful way—and participating in the "suspense" of experiencing the story again.

We can be more specific, however, in working out a sound understanding of "story," knowing that everyone knows what a story is—since we are all used to telling some kind of story to someone every single day—but stopping to understand what "makes a good story" is not often done.

Every story, for example, has a beginning, a middle, and an ending. In other words, it has a progression, moving from here—the starting point—to there, and then on to the ending. It is necessary to actually think in terms of these "sections" of anything that one wants to imbue with the power of story. A progression refers to a gradual "unfolding," meaning that it never gives away "where it is going" too soon. The various parts of the planned progression need to "emerge" at the appropriate point in the story's development. It has to be conceptualized and planned.

Each of the three "sections" of the story's development is important. A story has a "beginning," which invariably is a "setup" of some kind. The scene must be set. Location must be established. The action about to unfold has to be founded in some way.

Sometimes, it is a problem that is brought to the surface in the "beginning" of the story. Sometimes a key character is introduced, the one who will carry the story forward. But there has to be a setup in order for the beginning of the story to work.

The story has a middle. The "action" begins. Dimensions of the story come into conflict in some way. Characters clash. Something unexpected happens. We are here in the "middle" of the story; it is moving ahead; we are away from the setup, and we have a sense of what the "problem" of the story is, but we do not yet know where it is going or how it is all going to work out.

The story form, then, always has an "ending," a resolution. It plays itself through to a conclusion, or at least something that will bring closure to the story. Things "work out." Everything is resolved—often not in a big way, not with a "bang," since most "stories" play themselves out on a "small stage." Often the resolutions are negotiated, and life moves on from them without big jerks or abrasive clashes. They end with a sense of relief, rest, and a good feeling that "all is well" and that "we can all move on now." This progression, though, from beginning through the middle to a resolution is the essence of "story." Every sermon must have a progression for the potency of the "sermon form" to be carried into improvisational preaching.

Another characteristic of the story form is its visual quality. Media today have shaped human sensibility—and the media of the emerging century is almost all based in the sensory. You can "see and hear" what is going on, even if it is being told with words only. In old radio dramas of the 1930s and 1940s, this was a fine art. Words do fill the imagination of a hearer; with them we all create our own "pictures" in our own ways. This visual quality results, though, from a story's details. It is in the details where the difference between a weak and a strong story is found. For the story form to work, as for every story itself, the details have to be there, and they have to be highly visual—and carefully, sparingly, and vividly chosen.

The details of the story are not "judgments"—judgments do not work in a story. Good stories do not make pronouncements that something is "beautiful" or "terrifying" or "bad" or whatever. Details are *visual*, so that one gets a picture, a powerful picture in one's head—but not in a judgmental way. Someone in the story may be visually described as "elderly," or in greater detail, "over seventy"; the character may be "large and imposing, very round"—those are visual details—but one is not a "bad man" or a "beautiful woman"—those are judgments, not visual details. It is in the details that stories take on "flesh and bones" and reality. It is in the details where the power of the story lies. Details are description.

Stories conjure up not just an "idea," but also an "emotional" response to what is said. The best stories have a complex emotional fabric, often arising out of crises. It is the crisis where in "real life" we are confronted with not knowing what is going to happen next. Invariably, several different outcomes are possible—and all of them are not necessarily happy ones. Stories are emotional, and to tell our stories to others is to share our emotions. Stories really are designed to "move" the speaker as well as those with whom he or she shares them. By their very nature, they make us feel something, often something very elemental and profound. "Let me tell you about the day my sister found out she had cancer." The "outcome" of the story is already shared in advance; and yet the emotional power of the story to be told has a universal quality about it. That is how good, or great, stories work—and we all have a thousand of them within; few days go by that do not add another one to our story "file."

What the good storyteller knows very well, though, is that this emotional response does not come from the hearer *being told* how to respond; it arises from the circumstances and outcome of the story itself. In other words, the hearer's response to the story is "discovered" by the hearer in sharing the story.

Stories can have "points," of course, at the end, even a kind of "moral," though often the "point" or "moral" is not explicitly stated at all; it is left to be "found" by the story's hearer. Stories can even have a "go thou and do likewise" ending, but even when they are used in sermons—leaving the preacher to "talk about" the story that has just been told, hearers should be given credit for knowing how to understand and experience the story's pull for themselves.

Jesus, as we all know, told innumerable stories, probably many more than we even have record of in our Gospels; but he did not tell them just to entertain, though entertain they did. He told parables, those stories designed to carry meaning over and above the story itself; but meaning, nonetheless, that would not have been as vividly expressible in any other way. His parables were common stories, drawn from day-to-day activities of merchants, farmers, and women at their work.

What we learn from Jesus' stories about the use of stories in improvisational sermons is that stories are not told because they are good stories—which, very often, they are. Instead, they are told because they "mean" something. Jesus told parables—stories that spoke always of things beyond themselves. "A man went down that terribly dangerous road between Jerusalem and Jericho, and sure enough he was mugged along the way; robbed, beaten up, and left for dead. He could have lain there for days, despite the fact that other travelers noticed his body in the bushes as they passed." It is not just a story, though it is a very good, and very real story. But the story is told because it will rise above story to parable, to a figure of speech that will "say something" about human life, particularly life for those in the new kingdom of God. *How, then, shall we live?* is the question that hearers ask—and the preacher told them a story about "how to live." With this we begin to open up the "meaning" of story and storytelling in improvisational preaching.

Stories are not new—not at all. They are as old as humanity itself. They are, in fact, one of the two most ancient human art forms of which we have record, the other being various kinds of markings and cave paintings. Around campfires, to entertain each other, to teach the children, to motivate one another for difficult and dangerous tasks, to celebrate and build their own individual and collective identities, people told stories. With stories they charted the past as well as the future; with stories they marked out their values and ideal forms of behavior; with stories they passed dreams and aspirations from one generation to the next.

What makes the story form so unique and adaptable for the contemporary sermon is that every story—literally *every* story—has the ability to do five things simultaneously, something that virtually no other literary or speech form can do.

First, stories educate; they teach. This is not just a matter of a "teaching" story as opposed to some other kind. The fact is that nothing teaches better than a good story—and it does so because it does not set out to do so. What teaches best tries not to teach; and that's a good story. What do we learn from stories? We learn basic information. One character will teach another something—and we who share the story listen in; we overhear the information, and the power of that as a teaching tool is inestimable. But beyond that, stories teach habits, values, modes of thinking and doing, and outcomes, or consequences, of action. We learn because we watch and listen—and are influenced, often profoundly so. Our defenses are down. We absorb; and what we absorb, and often without knowing, becomes part of us.

Second, stories inspire. Granted, the word *inspire* is a slippery one. Homiletician and teacher David Schlafer likes to talk about Christians being "in-spirited." That is the idea here. Stories carry "spirit" within them—spirit that can often be "holy," but whenever it is upbeat and lifting, it plays a very positive part in human life. When the "Spirit" is from God, the story itself becomes "holy" and its power is often without measure. We have all heard "inspiring" or "inspirational" stories. Not cheaply done ones that play on emotions, but ones that speak of the "Spirit" of God coming alive. Stories provide an in-spiriting—and, at its best, that in-spiriting reflects a sharing of the Holy Spirit's work and activity. The stories may be mundane and extraordinarily human; they do not have to be about lofty "spiritual" matters. They can be about who we are, and how we touch each other, and how we reach out to each other, and how we carry each other—but in such stories the Holy Spirit also moves.

Third, stories create visions. This is not the same thing as inspiration. This is about imagining a future, conjuring up what "could be," or even what "will be," if we all put our shoulders together. What *could* my life be like—or your life? How could, in whatever small ways are imaginable, we actually touch and change the world? Often visions of what could be arise from stories even when we don't plan for them to, often when we do not even think that they might. This is because the process of imagining a future often arises from looking closely at the present, at things we have seen or done in the here and now. The seeds for constructing a better future, a better relationship or community are often brought to light only in the telling of a present story. And then we see it.

Fourth, stories entertain. This is not easy to talk about, since so few sermons these days seem to be concerned about it. Henry Mitchell, a great preacher and the best-known African American homiletician of the last century, told a group of preaching teachers a few years back that it was time to teach preachers to how to entertain in the pulpit. Because, he said, the opposite of entertaining is "BORING!"—it was his exclamation point and his capital letters.[2]

This is not entertainment in some crass sense, not in some joke-telling, trivializing sense. This is entertainment that causes everyone present to be riveted to what the preacher is doing and saying—and enjoying being riveted. It is entertainment that knows and enjoys humor, that understands that laughter, whether overt or covert, builds human community and spirituality. It is entertainment that also knows the value of being moved to tears. Needless to say, perhaps, few things are more flat-out entertaining than good stories. It is even possible to define the nature of entertainment itself as the telling of a story—whether in its comic form, its tragic form, or even in the combination form that Hollywood today calls the *dramedy*. And while the moving, entertaining story can be told in a thousand different media, from a radio play, to a television program, to a motion picture, to a good short story or novel, to a good biography, to a tale told from the back of a wagon to a group of kids. One of the ways a story can be told just as entertainingly is by a preacher from a pulpit or platform in a sacred space on a Sunday morning.

Finally, stories shape *behavior*. This means that a story has what it takes to prod somebody into doing something. Virtually every story that Jesus told had a "go thou and do likewise" either attached to it, or strongly implied in it. Sermons too often are little more than intellectual or even emotional exercises—except when sermons are shaped like stories, and they have motivational power. This does not mean that a story should tell people *what* to go do. In fact, most of the time that is precisely what it should *not do*. None of us likes to be told what to do. We prefer suggestions. We are open to ideas about what we might do, or might consider doing. Direct orders or even commands we are seldom attracted to; but ideas that prod us, or stories that give us guidance—those things we are very open to.

Let's illustrate this by looking at one story, drawn from my own background—a story that I have told as part of a past improvisational sermon.

> She was a friend of mine, a former student, one of those who makes a decision to keep in touch with the prof. She lived not far away in another suburb. I got to know her through two classes of mine that she was in over the course of a year and a half. She was Myra. Smart, a bit quiet, and sometimes very shy, but friendly and polite to a fault. Her personality was warm, and she was, truth be told, very likable.
>
> Myra was an artist; in fact, she was not a communication major at all, but an art major. I thought she was very good, and I let her know that. I went to her senior art show, which a local newspaper reviewer called "extremely promising."

Her abstracts, he wrote, are "both unsettling and hopeful at the same time."

The problem was that Myra suffered from manic depression so severe that it would leave her paralyzed through long stretches of time. In short, life, for Myra, was a roller coaster. When she was manic, she could conquer the world; her artistic output was prolific; when she was depressive— and it was always, it seemed to me, one way or the other— she was unable to work. Her schoolwork was always affected by her mood swings, which is always what brought her to the attention of her teachers.

Before I met Myra, her parents had sought psychiatric help for her, which she would alternate between liking and disliking. She went through any number of shrinks, as she called them. Someplace along the line, though, for reasons that I never learned, her parents cut off their support, and Myra was on her own, as she was when I first encountered her in one of my courses.

Right after she graduated, though, she managed to get a clerical job, one that didn't pay very much, but she seemed able to somehow get by. And she was determined to be the artist she always wanted to be, even though she had no idea how she would support herself in such an undertaking. She also faced up to her manic depression, and sought out—I think for only a few sessions to get over some hurdle—a shrink. She found him, I think, through the yellow pages: he was not far away from where she lived, and, as she said, his name sounded right. He was a psychologist, not a psychiatrist. He could counsel her, but not keep her on medications. But she wanted, and needed, to talk about her life and her illness. Somehow they would be brought under control together.

It was fairly expensive, but she knew it was important— and, remarkably, in retrospect, he took a liking to her. He was an elderly man, very large and imposing, whose last name was Nathan.

He spoke with a heavy accent, so heavy that at times he was difficult to understand. He would lean back in his large chair and rock slowly, his hands folded across his girth, listening, smiling ever so slightly.

I went with her to see Dr. Nathan only once, because she wanted me to meet him, and he had agreed to let me share a few minutes of one of their sessions. But their originally planned three sessions stretched out into weekly sessions. He adjusted his fee for her—even though she learned later that he did that for many of his patients. As he told her, his rich patients enabled him to see some who were not rich.

Obviously, despite the discount her bill grew; but she was deeply conscientious, and would pay him regularly whatever she could. And each month he would send a monthly statement. Invariably, the formal statement she received would have in it a short, hand-scrawled note, a thank-you note for whatever she had paid that month. The notes were always encouraging to her; they were clearly meant to be. Their sessions went on for more than two years, and it was very clear, as I would see her from time to time, that something—whether it was him or not I cannot say—was giving her focus and convincing her that, despite her mood swings, she could still be whatever she wanted to be.

Then a strange thing happened. Through a relative of hers, she got a job offer from a company that would require her to move across the country. It wasn't an art job, as she put it, but one that held out the possibility of letting her move in that direction. She wanted to take it. She felt ready. It became the topic of several of her weekly decisions as she mulled it over. He listened to her, and talked with her about the implications of it all. He also told her that she was ready, and she took the job.

The move was planned and made. I heard from her several times after she was relocated. She still had mood swings, but seemed to understand them better; she seemed to cope with them better. And even after the move, not surprisingly, she would send Dr. Nathan a payment like clockwork every month—whatever she could afford, even though, as before, sometimes the amounts were relatively small. Most of the time, she would enclose a letter to him, as he had urged her to do, explaining how things were going, how she was doing, and whether she was managing to do some artwork along the way. In one particular letter, she told him that she had an opportunity to work on her master's degree in art; and that she was hoping that somehow she could work that out. Each time, he would send her a handwritten note of encouragement and thanks with each monthly statement.

Then, one day when her statement arrived, the note was different—she shared it with me, with permission that I can share it with you. The note from Dr. Nathan read:

You write an interesting letter and I am glad that you are keeping in touch. It seems like a good move for you to complete your education and get a higher degree that will enable you to get a teaching position if you want it. Try not to push yourself to it too fast, why not enjoy it? I am gratified that you feel that I helped you. Of course it's extremely important to me to be of some use to others. However, you must not thank me for not rejecting you. Take it for granted that you are and will be accepted. You earned it and deserve it. As to payment in the future, you don't owe me anything. Use the money for painting materials. I'll be real happy if you do.

It was signed just "Nathan." That was what the note said. The amount of the bill, enclosed as always, had a heavy red line drawn through it. It was for $3,650.

Let's think about this story. Does it teach something? My judgment is that it does—it is a kind of parable that has a point within it. It is, at one level, a decent story; but it is more than that at the same time. It does not hit one over the head, but it says something specific and potent just as it is. Does it inspire? Again, I like the story because I think that it does. It is about a remarkable person, one whose actions have caused me to rethink my own. Does it create a vision? A vision of what? Perhaps of how things could be, or ought to be, a vision of an alternative way of looking at work and vocation and life? I think so; or at least I find that in the story. It is a story of understanding and human contact and compassion. Does it entertain? That is probably not the right word at all here; but it does have suspense, even tension, within it that holds us until we know how it comes out. That is the core of what entertainment is. It holds us until the end and catches us with a bit of delight when we find out what happened.

Is it behavioral in the sense in which we discussed that concept earlier? Does it suggest a pattern for living? A way of living life? I think it most certainly is. Someone behaves like that—someone unexpected, and with a lot of money at stake. The story calls to us to consider how we would act in that situation—and whether we would respond in the same way. What Dr. Nathan did was not just forgive a debt, as important as that was; but also it involved caring about another over time, even in a professional relationship. The call to act is in the story itself; it does not even have to be said. In fact, it is all the more poignant and powerful if it is left unsaid. Can this story find its place in an improvisational sermon? The answer is yes, emphatically yes.

At the other level that we talked about—what makes a story—look at the story of Myra and Dr. Nathan again. It has the three great characteristics of a good, dramatic story. It has progression, a beginning, middle, and end. The beginning introduces the characters and sets up the interaction that will develop; the middle presents the plot, the dilemma that both encounter in Myra's leaving, and how Dr. Nathan will respond to it; and the ending at first is expected, but then turns on an unexpected story shift.

The story also fills in enough details to create its reality; you can see and feel what is going on; in a very short space you get a sense of knowing what is going on. The details are spare and clean, and they work. And the story is emotional; it conjures up feelings, but lets us experience the feelings of both of its characters. We can empathize with both of them. There is pain and pathos, and we are invited to share it. There is a wrenching emotional release when the story comes to its ending, its denouement. We experience what has gone on. Such stories, though, are everywhere around us. The trick is to learn to see them, to recognize them at close range in the circle of our own lives, and to keep records of them so that they do not slip away from our memories.

Where, though, do we get such stories? Where do we find them, or how do we create them, if that is the right word? Look at it this way.

Storytelling has spawned what we have come to know as the *Chicken Soup* era. In itself, that is a wonderful metaphor, of course. Stories as chicken soup; chicken soup as story—soothing, goes down easy, warms you up, makes you well. Chicken soup is a wonderful metaphor for the story, even the story as part of the improvisational sermon. Everyone by now knows about this enormous, and still growing, industry. It started with a couple of books—collections of stories drawn from here and there—and now it knows no bounds: *Chicken Soup* radio and television program, *Chicken Soup* newspaper columns, now calendars, stationary, and who knows what else. And the books keep proliferating. *Chicken Soup* for teenagers, for the elderly, for the disadvantaged, for children—for veterans, which is the latest one I have seen. On and on. It is difficult to keep up with. People are buying stories, collections of stories, stories with morals, or happy endings.

Some preachers got on the *Chicken Soup* bandwagon early, since it was a whole new place to find sermon material. The only problem was that the stories those preachers were reading and bringing into their sermons were also being read at the same time by their parishioners. It was cute for a time—"we have read the same stories"—but it is not something that wears well from the pulpit. If people have already read the stories that the preacher tells on Sunday morning, then where is the interest and the freshness?

There is a message in those *Chicken Soup* books, though. It is that people are hungry for stories—common, down-to-earth stories. Not big, world-shattering stories, but the day-to-day stories of life and living. That is what is in those books. Moreover, with the success of the industry, most people who ever bought one of those books have probably gotten a card at some point asking them to submit a story for a future *Chicken Soup* book. That is how the *Chicken Soup* books are being written from this point on.

Honesty requires one to say, however, that for every good, moving, chicken soup story in one of those books or on TV, there are ten of those stories that are flat, clichéd, or silly; stories that lack both the ring and the poignancy of reality. We will usually work through those ten in order to get to that one that does work. But, still, it is canned soup. Of course we eat canned chicken soup. It's a fast-food, heat-it-up-and-eat-it world. It may keep us going, but it has little taste, and it is not nearly as good for us as we would like it to be. The same is true with chicken soup from a book. The stories are prepackaged, cooked in advance, and they sound and taste like it.

We all know the difference between soup from a can and homemade chicken soup. In fact, there is no comparison. Homemade soup is the real thing. It creates an aroma that can transform a house. It has nutrients that not only keep us going, but—as all of our grandmothers said—can cure whatever ails us. For the preacher, storytelling must be seen in the same way. So what is homemade chicken soup? It is the *preacher's own stories*. Not stories drawn from a book, whether a chicken soup book or some other illustration collection. We want to hear each other's stories. Done correctly, these are not egotistical recitations of "what happened to me this week." These are a preacher's careful watching and listening to life as he or she lives it.

For a couple of years in the late 1980s, I lived in east Tennessee, a few miles down the road from the little town of Jonesboro—the home of the National Storytelling Festival. It is week of nothing but tent upon tent of storytellers and storytelling every fall. It is storytelling heaven. I have no idea how many large crowds I was a part of those few fall seasons as we listened to the storytellers, great entertainers, all. But I came away with one very clear impression. Looking back, apart from how good a storyteller actually was, the stories that always evoked the most intense responses from the audiences were the stories that arose from the storyteller's own life and experience. For some reason, those stories had a spark and a sparkle that even the best storyteller could not achieve with a story he or she "read in an excellent book."

For preachers, the message could not be more pointed: Learn to find and tell your own stories. What is gradually dawning on those who wish to attract people, young or old, to both worship and preaching is that somehow the art of storytelling must be brought fully into play. Real stories of real people and situations connect to contemporary people. But make the stories you tell in your preaching the stories that have come from your own life and experience.

The biggest and most valid criticism of telling one's own stories is that they become very egotistical; and people quickly grow tired of hearing the preacher be a hero one more time this week. There is a simple rule, however, that prevents this from happening. It is that the preacher, or the storyteller, is *never* to be either the hero or the villain of the story. Granted, every story will be the storyteller's own story—meaning that he or she was there and saw what happened in the story. But the story is always, always, to be *about* somebody else. The preacher may be a character, a participant, in the story, but never the main character. The preacher's presence in the story can be visible, and the use of what he or she saw or heard need not be left out—but the preacher is the narrator, one who stands on the sidelines and observes what is going on. From that vantage point, the story can be told—and there is *never* any danger of that story being perceived as egotistical or self-based.

The story of Myra and Dr. Nathan is drawn from my experience. I watched the story develop; I knew both of them over time. And I was told some of the details of what happened, since I was very interested in their unusual relationship. It is my story. No one knows it or can tell it quite like I can; and I know that it is a true story. But it is not a story about me, though I am there on its edges. I narrate it, even to the point of giving it authenticity by recognizing my position in it. I am not its hero nor its main character. So in no way does it sound egotistical, even though it is my story. That is how all good stories are devised. They are not chicken soup stories that others might already have read. They are homemade soup stories—and the homemade part is what gives the story its particular flavor and poignancy.

How does one develop good stories *of one's own* for improvisational preaching—and how does one select just the right ones for a particular sermon? To use stories effectively in improvisational preaching, one must become a collector of stories. It must be done systematically and regularly. One does this by becoming an inveterate watcher of people. Become, in short, a keen observer of everything that goes on around you. Where does one look? The answer is that one watches for the points of crisis, occasionally large but more often than not, small crises, in which people find themselves. This becomes those places where people find themselves up against a wall, so to speak, and so must figure out what to do to get themselves or someone else out of a jam. Occasionally, these crises are small enough to result in little more than a profound embarrassment. Sometimes, though, they are much larger.

One is driving in traffic, and, like a good samaritan, gets out of the car to assist someone nearby in trouble; but when the good samaritan goes to get back in his car, he discovers, in traffic, that he has locked the keys in the car. It is a crisis. So what should—or will—one do? The situation may, in fact, get tense; and the observer may try to be a helping person in the situation, but still not succeed very well. One watches, not necessarily from the sidelines, and one makes notes because, one way or another, there will be some resolution to the story. The careful observer who will need a story for improv preaching will write down a half page of notes so that the story does not slip away.

Such stories are everywhere; they are the daily stuff of human life, whether in interactions with strangers, with family members, with coworkers or colleagues on the job, or even in the dynamics of church life. No two experiences or crises are alike. All have emotional dimensions, all have meanings beyond themselves, and all are worth telling for their parabolic value. For preaching purposes, one should plan to collect one such story a day, writing out a summary of what happened, along with details about names, sights, sounds, colors, and so on, that might give the story life and drama. A simple stenographer's notebook usually provides all one needs to become a collector and user of stories—the essential ingredient for the potent improvisational sermon.

How does one select and use a story in a sermon? The criterion for selecting a particular story of one's own for the sermon will usually *not* be whether the story is a good one or not. That will be important, though not necessarily pivotal. What will be pivotal is whether the story's meaning—usually its parabolic meaning—actually fits what one wants the sermon, overall, to say. As we shall see in our final chapter, when we construct a sermon, we do, indeed, want it to say something—and we have to know pretty certainly what that something is before we start preaching. When we do get a sense of that, then we will go looking in our story notebook or collection for a story whose meaning points in that direction as well. The matches will make the difference between a sermon that is most powerful in its overall effect, and one that is good, if not strongly on target.

Before we turn to look at Bible-based stories for our improvisational sermons, and then at the process of preparing a sermon in the shape of a story, we need to offer some necessary cautions about the use of stories in sermons—cautions that concentrate on mistakes in storytelling usually made by those just starting out on improvisational preparation and preaching. There are at least a half dozen of these common *problems* with learning to tell one's own creative, invariably fascinating, stories—the kinds of stories that can readily be used as parables and behavioral models in the sermon.

The first problem is that what one plans to be one story easily turns into two or three—and the initial story's focus is lost. Stories, in short, run together. The rule is very simple: make sure you have and use only one story at a time. While the rule is simple, sometimes carrying it out is not. This is because while our lives, on any given day, are an unceasing set of stories, they all run together. We go from thing to thing as the day unfolds—the drive to work with other annoying cars, the early morning encounter with some distressed colleagues, the telephoned news from family far away that a relative is very ill. And so on. It is all continuous, and we seldom stop to notice the seams. Telling a story of any one thing from that day requires, though, that it be lifted out from the rest, and that it have a clear starting and stopping point. Stories should not, as often happens, be run together. Knowing how and when to stop a story is one of the first things to be learned as a storyteller.

Second, it is not uncommon for new storytellers to leave out key chunks of a good story, chunks that are set up by the story but then passed over, prompting the hearers to wonder what happened there. For example, one tells a story about the mending of a long feud between the teller and a grandparent. Then, at a crucial point in the story the teller says that after such-and-such happened "he accepted me again." The story sounds fine, and interesting; but at that "accepted me" line, the hearer is left hanging. *How* did he accept you? What happened to let you know you were accepted? We know he accepted you, but tell us, specifically, what took place. A chunk of the story is missing—and the hearer feels cheated. One wants to press the storyteller to finish the story and, as a child often says, don't leave out any good parts. It is a common problem in learning to tell a story of one's own.

Third, the *setup* of stories is often weak; sometimes overlooked entirely. Good stories are not just told; they are built. And the building of the story requires a foundation, a setting of the stage, a few careful lines of "once upon a time *when*"—and the "when," expanded a bit, provides the setup, the opening. "It was mid-morning and very hot outside. It had rained earlier in the day and I was still very wet. I didn't want to stop at the bank that morning, but I had no choice. Not only that, but the parking lot was full and I had to park what seemed like a quarter mile away. I was irritable, and not at all prepared for what I was going to find when I walked into the bank that morning." That is a setup. The story will emerge from what I saw unfold in the bank. The setup is both simple and crucial. Every story needs one.

Fourth, the storyteller does not build the story from details that enhance it and make it vivid. Details, carefully chosen, specific and easy to see with the mind, are what bring stories to life. We talked about details themselves earlier, and here we need to add to those details the give and take of real dialogue. In stories, people talk, and storytellers learn to hear that talk and, to some extent, replicate it in the telling of the story. Every good storyteller knows this. "And then he said. . . . And then she turned around and said to him. . . . Then they walked down the stairs side by side, with him saying over and over again. . . ." Fill in those dialogue blanks.

The hearer must be able, mentally and emotionally, to *see* and *hear* what is going on in the story. "The boy looked to me to be about twelve or thirteen, wearing overalls and dirty, oversized tennis shoes. He sat on the curb at the street with his head buried in his hands. You could tell he was trying to cover up his crying.

Finally, he stood up quickly, thrust both fists into the air and shouted into the night—" Shout it, let the hearer hear it. The storyteller learns how to do this with simple, selected details. Can you see what is going on? This is how we are able to experience what is going on. Nothing is more powerful, nothing bridges biblical truth into the present better than great story details and dialogue, told with—and only with—an improvisational style that can penetrate to the heart of every person in the room.

Fifth, stories are often too sanitized by novice storytellers. We not only can handle, but also we *want* stories that are real, stories that cut though the surfaces and show us real things. I once had a retired high-ranking police officer in a storytelling class, a man who had served in a gang unit in Los Angeles; he was going into the ministry. He had a knack for storytelling, and we all knew that he had a thousand stories from the unusual life that he had lived. But he would start a story and then say something like, "but that would be too much to tell you." Invariably, his peers would press him: "Tell us; we can handle it, and we would like to know." Finally, he would. And it would be a richly textured story of real life—unsanitized, told in a gritty and moving way, as only he could tell it.

The sixth problem is a little more complex, but very important, nonetheless. It is that storytellers often provide their own reactions to their stories as they tell them—instead of just telling the story and letting hearers react on their own. For example, the storyteller describes a particular behavior and then adds, "I was just appalled when he did that." No. Storytellers just *tell* the story. No more, no less. No personal commentary or asides, at least not during the story. The hearer is the one who may or may not be appalled at a particular turn that the story takes. But it is not the role of the storyteller to coach the hearer on how to react, even in a sermon. In fact, one of the beauties of storytelling, particularly improvisational storytelling, is that it allows those who share the story to react in many different ways. And that is how it should be.

Notes

1. Leonard Sweet, *SoulTsunami: Sink or Swim in the New Millenium Culture* (Grand Rapids: Zondervan Publishing House, 1999), 424.

2. Henry H. Mitchell, "Preaching in the Third Millenium: A Theological Word Toward Survival," in Academy of Homiletics, Papers of the 32nd Annual Meeting, Oakland, California, 49.

CHAPTER FOUR

THE BIBLE: IMPROVISATION'S GREAT SOURCE

Few things are more important to contemporary preaching—to improvisational preaching—than bringing the Bible fully to life and meaning. Given the unique power of stories today, we will urge that the Bible be preached in a story-based fashion; still, the answer to "what to preach" in contemporary worship is unambiguous: we are to preach the Bible. It is our source as Christian preachers, traditional *or* contemporary. In contemporary preaching, however, young preachers can easily lose track of the Bible in the pulpit or on the platform. It is deeply tempting today to talk about relationships, the problems of growing up or getting along or forming families, and to do it more from today's self-help books than anything else. So we have to hear the call for us, in improvisational preaching, to *stick close to the Bible,* to see that what we say in our sermons, even about relationships, grows directly out of Holy Scripture.

In short, preaching is nothing if it is not biblical—thoroughly, accurately, intensely, uncompromisingly biblical. Paul's urging to

Timothy to "preach the word" may not mean today exactly what the words meant when they were originally written, but the similarity is unmistakable. It takes work to preach the Bible, however; one should have no illusions about that; and when we realize that our preaching of the Bible today needs to be shaped into story forms, the task is not nearly as easy as it might appear on the surface.

Biblical illiteracy, particularly among young people and even young Christians, is one of the true problems confronting the future of the church. One of the few opportunities that exists for work on this problem is for today's young contemporary preachers to preach Scripture and its stories. The Bible is an enormous two-part book made up of sixty-six individual "books" or documents, some historical, some history, some biography, some didactic or prophetic, some poetic, some just plain old letters, some that sound more like science fiction or fantasy than anything else. As easy as it is to say "preach the word," meaning, for us, "preach the Bible," actually doing that, and doing it with integrity, is one of the most difficult and daunting tasks that the young contemporary preacher faces. Yet in many ways the future of the church rests on a new generation of preachers who will "tell the stories of the Bible," making clear their meanings and their lessons.

The Bible is the improvisational preacher's great storybook. It is filled with literally hundreds of stories about God, God and humans interacting, human beings trying to come to terms with God; stories of Jesus Christ, God's Son, becoming flesh and coping with human life and experience, Jesus living in a way that "teaches us" how to live and be as God wills in the world, Jesus facing and overcoming death in his resurrection—and on and on. Stories are everywhere; and where things are not given to us overtly as "story," we find materials with which we can constantly create new stories that breathe life into poems, aphorisms, backgrounds, and expectations. If storytelling is the ultimate form of improvisational speech, then the Bible is the ultimate "source book" for improvisational preaching. It is that straightforward and simple. In this chapter, we shall look closely at how to "tell" the story, and the stories, of the Bible.

Preach and Teach—Tell—the Bible's Stories

Unlike some holy books of other religions, which are didactic in style and content from beginning to end, the Bible is packed full of stories. The rabbis of old relished their stories, and the Old Testament is nothing if not a storybook. Granted, there are a few other kinds of writing there, but even within and behind those other "writings" there are stories. The rabbi of old would be asked a question, to which he would invariably reply, "That reminds me of a story—" Or, "Let me tell you a story—." With that, the stories of Abraham, Isaac, and Jacob are told in lavish detail, as are the stories of Joseph, Elijah, Samuel, Saul, and David. In between are the stories of the lesser known, but still important characters, from the Judges, including Gideon, Deborah, and Samson to the Prophets like Jeremiah, Isaiah, Ezekiel, and Daniel.

As we said a moment ago, it is important to realize how little known even these mainstream Old Testament stories are. The story of Joseph, for example, which is told in enormous detail and occupies the last long section of the book of Genesis, is a remarkably candid and even a contemporary story, filled with detail and imagery; and its meanings are startlingly clear, even in the telling. The story can be broken up into numerous pieces, each one a stand-alone story—and each one still needed today. Joseph's odd relationship with his father, the animosities with his brothers, his powerful temptations, his imprisonment, his climb up the Egyptian governmental hierarchy, and his extraordinary reunion with his family. What incredible stories! And they can be found on every page of the Old Testament in some form. They are stories alive for telling—the very grist for improvisational preaching.

At the heart of the New Testament as well are its stories. The stories of the Gospels and Acts are not nearly as well known as they ought to be; even the stories of Jesus' life and ministry are only vaguely known, at best, among today's young people. The birth stories are largely known only in their Christmas trappings. The miracle stories are known only in a vague mythic sense—yes, Jesus walked on water, didn't he? And his parables, his own numerous stories, remain unknown both in their details and in their meanings.

Then there are the remarkable stories of the Acts of the Apostles, the stories of the people who led the founding of the church in Jerusalem, including Barnabas, Peter and John, Stephen, Philip, and others. Then, of course, the great stories of Paul the apostle, whose life is traced with such vividness and care through the last two thirds of the Acts document. Ironically, some of the very best stories of those formative, opening decades of Christianity are told only when one "connects the dots," as it were—connecting Paul's letters to the circumstances and situations as they are told in Acts.

One ought to begin, to be sure, with what we might designate as the "mainstream stories," those that require only a retelling, since they are told in such sparkling detail within the pages of the Bible itself. Whether from Old Testament or New, preach the great stories. Invariably, for almost all of us, this requires that after we have selected one, we must read it again and again, taking notes, learning its details—often details that have escaped us until we come to the point of our own close examination. The story of Joseph and Potiphar's wife, David's war with Saul, Deborah and Barak saving the people, Esther saving the people, Jonah saving a different people, the story of Jesus' turning water into wine at Cana of Galilee, the somewhat problematic story (told twice in the Gospels) of Jesus driving money changers and other merchants from the Temple; preach the mainstream stories, the stories with just enough familiarity to require particularly careful telling. This is because some to whom you preach will know "about" these stories, whether they actually *know*, or remember, any of their details or not. Most likely, though, you will be telling the story in a way that brings it to new life for everyone to whom you speak.

In your use of the mainstream or somewhat familiar stories, do not read the entire story from the biblical text, and then in your sermon tell the entire story a second time. That is not necessary and uses up too much valuable time. Study and tell the story improvisationally in your own words; or, what is often better, read a part of the story, usually its opening paragraph or paragraphs to give people the sense of its biblical origins, and then pick up and tell the rest.

The great joy and insight of telling and teaching—preaching—the mainstream stories of the Bible is not in the celebration of the heroic men and women of the Bible, whether celebrating their greatness or their foibles, though there is a place for that. The insight, rather, is in telling about the *relationships* of the heroes and villains with both God and the people around them. Look particularly for relationships, those points at which the lives of two or more people, often all people of God, intersect, those moments when decisions of one affect the others. This is true not just in the "real stories" themselves, stories even of Jesus, but it is true as well in the stories told *by others*, even Jesus himself. The most meaningful, and usually the stories from which we learn the most are those that implicate us as we stand in the roles of various characters whose lives intersect in a given story. Most biblical stories, fortunately, are relational stories, so even though you focus on one character today and next week a different character, you build the story around the nature of the relationships. They have ways of speaking volumes to us about the living of our own lives before God and in community.

Preach and teach what we might call the "out of stream" stories from the Bible. There are countless of these in both the Old and the New Testaments. These are the stories of the "minor" characters, characters who play the all-important "supporting roles" to the giants, the lead characters. At this moment, you may not even be able to call the names of any of them; most of them, at least in the Old Testament, have names, though a few are nameless. In the telling of the mainstream stories, we mention one or two, since they pop up. But in case after case, they are real people with stories of their own.

For example, in the great Moses epic, there is the remarkable story of Jethro, Moses' father-in-law; he is a supporting character, but in his visit to Moses, bringing Moses' wife and children to visit him in the desert, he cannot help but observe what Moses is doing, and he and Moses have a conversation about it. Jethro makes a suggestion to his son-in-law that Moses takes to heart and follows, and the whole way of the great leader's dealing with his followers changes as a result. It is a great story—of Moses, yes, but particularly of Jethro.

The Old Testament is filled with Jethro stories. You only find them by reading the great stories. Read the story of Joseph from beginning to end, taking notes on the supporting cast, some of whom are critically important to "turns" in the story, some of whom are not named but identified in other ways. Read the story of David from beginning to end, doing the same thing. Takes notes on the supporting cast. Find Barzillai, and look closely at where he appears in the story (several places) and then piece together his life and his relationship to David and the people surrounding the king. The story of Barzillai is classic and profoundly instructive in an unforgettable way. Here, for example, is a way to tell the Barzillai story:

> He was an old man, eighty years old; and while we do not know very much about him, it is clear from what we do know that he was someone you would think was quite extraordinary. But a normal man—not an official, not someone with rank. He was a prosperous man, we know that, probably from a life of hard work—mostly, it appears,

as a farmer. He had heard that his king and a small army were in his region on something like an emergency expedition—what, he did not know. Except that he knew they were out in the barren, semiforest areas, their work was taking longer than they expected, and they had come without many provisions. So he and two of his friends loaded a couple of wagons with provisions and headed off to find them—which they did. With them they had cots for more comfortable sleeping, some dishes and cleaning supplies; and food, lots of food, wheat, barley, corn, beans, butter, honey, those sorts of things—enough for the men to be taken care of, a good stretch of time.

The old man's name was Barzillai. When the work of the king and his men was done—and it was a bitter work that left the king heartbroken but victorious, they started back home. Word had a way of getting out, and old Barzillai decided that he would go and meet the party on its way and go with it until it reached the last river before heading back into the city. When he reached the party, the king greeted him warmly, remembering all of the provisions that Barzillai had assembled for them. Then the king surprised Barzillai with a proposal:

"Come with me to the city and to the palace, and I will see that you have everything you need for the rest of your life. It is the least that I can do to repay what you did for me and my men."

Barzillai protested, though; but in the most gentle sort of way. He told the king that he probably didn't have much longer to live, and that his faculties were pretty much gone. In Barzillai's remarkable words, as we have them from the records, he said, "Can I discern what is pleasant and what is not? Can your servant taste what he eats or what he drinks? Can I still listen to the voice of singing men and singing women?" (2 Sam 19:35). He would, he told the king, be nothing but a burden. What he preferred, he said, was just a chance to walk along with the king for a little while—until they reached the river; and then Barzillai said that he would prefer to turn around and go back home. He did not mean to be disrespectful, or to give the impression of not appreciating his king's sincere invitation. But he said that he would prefer—and this is how he said it—he would prefer to go home and die in "my own town, near the graves of my father and my mother" (2 Sam 19:37). The king clearly was moved by Barzillai's expression both of appreciation and loyalty to his family.

But—but—then it was Barzillai's turn to make a request of the king. A young man named Chimham had been accompanying Barzillai; it is not clear whether they were related, whether he was Barzillai's son—probably not—or just a young servant boy who meant a lot to Barzillai. But at that moment, Barzillai took Chimham by the hand and, well, introduced him to the king.

"Let Chimham go with the king in my place," Barzillai said, "and do for him whatever seems good to you."

The king was surprised, but it was a deal. Chimham, the young servant, would reap the reward that the king had offered to the old man. When they reached the river, the king kissed Barzillai, bade him a thankful farewell, and watched as he turned around to slowly head home. Barzillai bade Chimham, his young servant, farewell; and turned a couple of times to wave as the young man became a part of the king's entourage, crossing the river into the great city and palace of the king.

Related to these stories are what we can call the "hidden stories." These are not about the minor figures or supporting cast, like Jethro and Barzillai. These are the stories of people who are clearly there in biblical text, but people whose stories are never overtly told; we know them only by inference and implication. They are stories that, if we dig and ferret and imagine in an inspirational way, we can get to know. While the Old Testament gives us a stellar cast of "out of stream" stories, the New Testament gives us an intriguing cast of hidden characters with their own stories.

Ironically, the story of Timothy, as important as he is in the New Testament, is one of these hidden stories. What do we know about him beyond his hometown, the names of his mother and grandmother, and that he became very important to Paul? No one, not even Paul, ever takes time to tell us Timothy's story; in this very real sense, he is hidden from us. What, though, can we discover about him? Are we able to piece together some dimensions of his story ourselves? Truly we can, if have the patience and the determination in our Bible study to work at it. What could be better in our preaching to young people than to explore, and tell, a, if not the, Timothy story? Ironically, the list of names of young men who surrounded Paul is profoundly interesting, and what we are saying about Timothy we could say about any of them, even though the information with which we work will be sketchier than with Timothy, who stands at the top of the apostle's list.

Who, for example was Demas—and what do we know about him? We will have to check a concordance just to see the texts where his name actually appears. But what comments about him give us clues to his nature, his relationship to Paul, and the momentous and deeply instructive decisions he made? Even piecing together the great hidden story of Onesimus the slave calls from us the best Bible study that we can carry out. Tell the hidden stories; but do not do so in a halfhearted or unprepared way. Do the work necessary to piece together not so much what we do know about the characters, but what we might know about them. Many of them play strikingly important roles in the stories of Jesus, or Peter, or, particularly, Paul. Do not get fanciful or overly cute. Be straight, in the way that a good television documentary on that character might seek to discover who he or she was, and what he or she did.

It is a kind of divine detective story in some cases. Bring the characters to life based on what clues you can find in the Bible, whether it is Jude or Titus or, as I have done in my book *Preaching Without Notes*, John Mark. Never forget that you are studying Holy Scripture in this undertaking, and that the goal is not just an illumination of biblical people and things, but a search for the truth, for the gospel, surrounding the people and their God, as well as their crucial dealings with each other.

Preach Stories of Biblical Backgrounds

The stories of what are sometimes called biblical backgrounds also need to be studied and told from the improvisational pulpit. This, too, is an important part of restoring biblical literacy; but the stories of people and events can only be fully appreciated and learned when we know where they came from and how they were shaped. Just as we said earlier that people, particularly young people, have an innate desire to learn, they are often deeply interested in where the Bible came from, and where it was all played out so many years ago. We need to break this down, as we did in talking about the Bible's stories, into several different kinds of material that are important and particularly adaptable to the improvisational sermon.

People do want to know the circumstances that produced the Bible books from which the preacher draws; and, in that sense, another kind of holy detective work kicks in. Here, the questions that serve as a guide to the preacher's work are fundamental. Who wrote this text, and what authorial problems do we know about? Tradition may tell us a specific author, and one may accept that as one wishes, but the question that would prove of both interest and instruction would have to do with whether scholars have in any way challenged or questioned the tradition.

This is not a matter of questioning the Bible in order to explore textual backgrounds; in fact, they are not the same thing at all.

We can indeed believe in and affirm the divine inspiration of Holy Scripture and still acknowledge the historical nature of the sacred book that has come to us via the mysterious activities of God. The New Testament, for example, was put together by a grand host of holy people, some intimates of Christ Jesus himself, some his disciples of an emerging new generation after him. Their books, collected into the Scriptures, were devised and written out of, and often in response to, specific circumstances, circumstances that we can infer, some with remarkable specificity, because of the evidence that has been passed along to us in Scripture. All of this is great fun to do, and fun to listen to when it is handled imaginatively.

So our study for the preaching of a text invariably begins with, who wrote it and under what circumstances. This is study, more-over, not only as background in our preparatory work on the ser-mon, but also it is study that should also find its way *into* our sermon; in fact, it often should become an important piece of the sermon itself. Our path through the exploration of biblical back-grounds from which we will prepare the sermon should become part and parcel of the sermon itself. Where we have been in preparation is precisely where we should often take those who listen to us. We play the role in a sense of tour guide, an orientation to public speak-ing that lends itself marvelously to our improvisational orientation.

What particularly motivates this, however, is that today's con-gregations, and younger ones in particular, are deeply interested in, even fascinated with, going behind the scenes of whatever they are working on. Where did something come from? How did it get to be like this? Who made it, and how? How was the movie put together? Are we able to watch the making of this music video? Take us there.

For younger people—and no doubt older ones too in our time—who look however slightly at religion and religious issues, those same questions hold a unique power. Where did a particular text come from, or, how did it come to be written? Put another way, what was going on that this text was, in some sense, a reply, or a response to? While these kinds of questions are often shadowy at best, sometimes with serious study we can come up with very good suggestions about answers. It is one thing, in today's world, to present a biblical text with the attitude of "take it or leave it," there it is, and that is how I will preach it; it is quite a different thing to present a text and try to explore what is behind it—not only its origins, but *why* it was important at the time it was written. This leads directly to a discussion of why it is still, or might still be, important today. This is the kind of material that can be turned into superb improvisational biblical work for presenting the gospel's message.

Not only are the circumstances or backgrounds of texts important for today's improvisational preaching, but so also is a close look at the *books* of the Bible themselves—as a part of a text's background, but also as writings in themselves. Every book of the Bible, again both Old and New Testaments, has a remarkable story—one that can be found in any good Bible encyclopedia. This is background of a remarkable kind. Where did this book come from? What do we know about its author and the circumstances that not only produced it, but that enabled it to become part of Holy Scripture?

In years past, young people in church were required, through camp or Vacation Bible School experiences, to learn the books of the Bible, in order, and often in their various sections, meaning the five books of Hebrew law, the books of history, poetry, and prophecy, and, in the New Testament, the Gospels, the Acts, and so on. Few young people today, even those actively reared in the church, know the Bible in this sense. Ask most of them to locate 1 Chronicles 10:5, and they will start by finding the Table of Contents in the front of the Bible, and searching out page numbers, not even sure whether what they are looking for is in the Old Testament or the New. It is a problem that requires the contemporary preacher's attention.

Preach Stories of Biblical Lifestyle

The Bible is also filled with stories of what we might call lifestyle. It all begins with the gospel stories of how Jesus himself lived. On numerous occasions, Jesus urged, "Follow me," and we may take that as a kind of universal command: We are to follow what Jesus taught and how he lived. Even Paul said at one point, "Follow my example, as I follow the example of Christ" (1 Cor 11:1 NIV). The question, though, to be consciously and deliberately dealt with is what that means; what does it mean if we say we are going to follow Jesus. The answer need not be treated as some esoteric or even spiritual notion; it can, and should, be treated as a matter of living, or lifestyle. If we are Christian, how are we to live? How are we to behave? What are we to give our lives to? These are questions that are of real interest to young people, growing up fast. It is the preacher who is called on to illumine the various demands that such a call to faith places upon the young Christian. Moreover, because of the nature of this down-to-earth material, it has to be handled in story, as story-telling, and as improvisational teaching via storytelling.

Ironically, it is in what we can call the aphorisms of living, first from the lips of Jesus himself, but even in the numerous ones found throughout the letters of Paul. Because they are aphorisms, or even single terms or concepts, they are all pithy, single statements. The Beatitudes of Matthew 5, for example, are among the very best of such sayings. "Blessed are the pure in heart, for they will see God." What does that mean? How may we open it up, drawing on other texts and stories, without losing the focus on that incredible rich and somewhat mysterious line? The aphorism tells us, in short, that an important part of the ethic of the kingdom of God is that we learn to live in a "pure in heart" manner. Or, "blessed are the meek," or those who "hunger and thirst after righteousness." All of these lines are part of building a way of living, in a sense; and it is the preacher who is charged with the responsibility for breaking open these beautiful, and very challenging, nuggets.

How are these broken open? By looking deeply into Jesus' own life and work—but also (we have to say) by thinking back to the previous chapter; there we set out looking for stories, parables, drawn from the world going on around us. In other words, where do we look today to see someone acting in a meek manner? Find that event, or incident, and the person behind it—and tell the story that you see. This may seem far-fetched, but it works. I can find countless people, many of whom I know and some I do not know but only encounter, who do, in fact, provide often unintended demonstrations of those beatitudes of Jesus.

Many stories are about forgiveness; and even though there are wonderful stories of forgiveness in both the Old and New Testaments, it is also true that if we watch what goes on around us we will also see forgiveness—real forgiveness—in action. The story I shared about Myra and Dr. Nathan is such a story that sheds light on the aphorisms of Jesus.

Aside from the list of beatitudes, the Gospels are filled with red-letter aphorisms of Jesus, even though one has to develop a keen eye to see them. For example, the Lord's Prayer is a series of aphorisms, too, though we seldom read it that way. Preaching or teaching it line by line, in separate sermons, is an extremely useful undertaking. "Give us this day our daily bread," means what? Is "our daily bread" our food, or is there more to it than that? The line may very well refer to our food, but in a time and place, and among people, for whom food was a relatively scarce commodity. Is that true in our day and time, and in the places where we live? What should one say about the portions served in today's restaurants, or what happens to the leftovers we leave behind after a sumptuous meal? What might Christ say about such a common situation for most of our lives? Meditate, and preach after meditating on—and studying—Jesus' words about praying for our daily bread. Find stories from the Bible, and from the present, that will bring these great teachings into living, breathing guidance for today's young people.

"Lead us not into temptation"—what does that mean? Consider the various possibilities. Or, again, "forgive us our debts or trespasses, as we forgive those who trespass against us." The possibilities for thinking, studying, exploring, and even playing with such a rich thought from the mouth of Jesus are almost endless. Translate such teachings into the stories that are everywhere—about Jesus' own temptations, about Peter's temptations, about Paul's own temptations and even failures; and about the stories of people struggling with temptation today. If you look for such stories, you will find them.

The letters of Paul, too, are shot through with aphoristic concepts and notions, any one (or series) of which is more than worth opening up in rich, provocative sermons. Concepts like those in Paul's list of the fruits of the Spirit may be unloaded for preaching, a concept at a time. When that is done, however, it should not be just a topical sermon on love, or joy or peace. Because these words are all found within a particular setting, they should be handled, one by one, in the context they appear. In this case, it means that one looks at the notion of joy as a fruit of having the Holy Spirit within one. How do you know you have the Holy Spirit? You know so if you are a joyful person, and the sermon revolves around what it means to be that kind of individual. The same with the other items as well.

Wherever one looks in Paul's richly human letters, his teaching about how to live as a Christian spills out on page after page. Some of the letters are heavily theological, of course, and yet many are profoundly practical; and in preaching we can explore the nature of Christian lifestyle, whether in our dealings with each other within the church, or in how we relate to people in normal life outside of the confines of the sanctuary.

Of all the aphorisms in the New Testament that call for careful and even sustained exploration is the one that appears first in the Sermon on the Mount: "Love your enemies." It is the aphorism of great reversal, as Jesus himself makes clear, prophetic, and radical:

"You have heard that it was said, 'You shall love your neighbor and hate your enemy.' But I say to you, Love your enemies" (Matt 5:43-44). The questions and issues for preaching burst from that line, landing almost always in a very real and gritty and practical world of living human beings. What is an enemy? How do I know when I have one? Is there any way to avoid having them? If my government tells me that "we" have enemies, what does that mean, and does Jesus' aphorism have anything to do with that? Beyond such basic questions to which the preacher should attend, there are others that have to do with what it means to love an enemy. What kind of behavior is implied in such a directive? How does one do that? What are barriers to doing that, and how might those barriers be overcome—that is, if they should be overcome? There is rich biblical preaching to arise from such concise, fervent texts.

Finally, preaching biblical ethics or morals is also a matter of exploring the very pattern of Jesus' life itself, not so much what Jesus says, or said, but what Jesus *did*, how he lived. This is a dimension of Bible study that also requires a keen and spiritual eye. It is Jesus living life and then implicitly saying, "Go and do likewise." Ironically, it is this orientation to the Bible that tends to focus us on what I take to be the single most difficult matter in all of the New Testament. That is, that Jesus laid down his life, as we are taught, for us—can we say he laid down his life for his enemies? Is this actually a part of the "follow me" directive? If it is, then how does it translate into how we live our lives? We know how Jesus laid down his life for us, and we even spend a good deal of time in our preaching and teaching letting people know that; but did Jesus mean for that to provide a model or a guide for how we are supposed to live as well? It may very well be—and it is the preacher's responsibility to call people to a "lay down your life" lifestyle.

Not only is it important for congregations of contemporary people, particularly young people, to know the Bible, but *just as important*—and I say that deliberately—is that one preach and teach the historical dimensions of the biblical eras themselves. It is, at one level, a matter relating to that most intriguing of topics: where did the Bible come from, and how did it come into being? At another level, though, it is a matter of understanding the historical currents and circumstances in which the various books and writings of the Bible were produced. Take a book like Ezra or Nehemiah from the Old Testament, closely related writings. It is impossible to read and understand them without pursuing an understanding of the Babylonian captivity of the Hebrew people. When did it take place? What were the circumstances that led up to it? Who were the various peoples involved in it? What role or roles did Ezra and Nehemiah play? There are stories everywhere here—and one can teach, inspire, and motivate by turning these materials into excellent stories for improvisational preaching.

Or take a New Testament book like the magnificent Revelation. It was not produced in a vacuum at all. As we have already indicated, it confronts us with initial questions: who wrote it, which John was it, or can we even know for certain that someone named John wrote it? We know that it was written from exile, from a secure Roman prison. But what can we say about its larger historical circumstances? Who is the emperor, and how might we be able to tell? What is this emperor's story? For the writer, a Christian who wants to get a document out of prison and successfully into the hands of people in various churches, what problems of circumstance and logistics must he overcome? Where does the book of Revelation fall in the historical story of the Bible? How did those who constructed the canon of the New Testament, the final list of books that were to become Christian Scripture, understand the book of Revelation to be Holy Scripture? All of these kinds of background, or historical questions (and countless others) are important to aid *how* shall we interpret the message of the book.

To talk, in short, about preaching and teaching the Bible means to tell the Bible's stories and narratives, even though that is often as far as preaching the Word ever gets. But we still have not exhausted the program for preaching and teaching the Bible. We need to go one more important step beyond the Bible's stories and biblical origins or backgrounds; we need to go as well into the preaching and teaching of biblical doctrines and theologies.

Preach Church Stories of Doctrine

The most difficult stories to find and tell—as important as they are—are stories that explain Christian doctrine and theology. This is much more esoteric. You can teach doctrine as catechism: what do we believe about baptism, about the Lord's Supper, about the nature of salvation, about the nature of the Second Coming of Christ? As these ideas are elaborated, they become this church's or that church's theology. Granted, biblical doctrines and theologies vary widely from denomination to denomination, and even within various breakouts within denominations; even the priority of biblical doctrines can vary significantly from congregation to congregation. Despite such differences, however, the preaching of Bible doctrine and theology is very important to improvisational preaching.

Some basic doctrines are so fundamental to the history and practice of the Christian faith that they run across all denominational lines, despite their variations. Invariably, the doctrines have concrete, often elaborate meanings. For example, the doctrine of baptism is vital to all Christianity, regardless of where one's denomination or fellowship falls on the spectrum of belief concerning the doctrine. The point, though, is that even young people possess, as they should, a curiosity about "our beliefs"; what do we believe about baptism—and why? How are our beliefs about baptism, say, connected to the Bible, and even to particular biblical texts? Why do we believe in infant baptism, or adult baptism? Why this particular form of baptism as opposed to some other? And what is the purpose and meaning of baptism? What happens to us when we are baptized? Anything? Or is it just something that we do, a rite of entry into a particular religious group? Exploring from the Bible questions like these is to preach, as we should from time to time, doctrinally.

The same can be said about the doctrine of the Lord's Supper, called various things, such as the Eucharist or the communion service. Many young Christians, particularly those who have had no exposure to or participation in any catechetical instruction, know virtually nothing about such an important doctrine, again one that stands near the center of the Christian church's life. What do the biblical texts on the sacrament, or ordinance (again called different things by different groups) actually say? Can the preacher preach on those texts, relating them in some clear fashion to the practices of the fellowship itself? Who can partake of the sacrament, and how is it to be done? How often is it to be done? Again, as with baptism, what is supposed to happen when one participates in it? How do our practices concerning it relate to the biblical text?

The questions, though, are specific as they relate to what we are saying here. These are difficult matters to turn into stories, as I am contending here that they should be. But there is an excellent potential strategy for the improvisational preacher. These are matters that are more than just biblical, since the formative elements of both doctrine and theology are found in church and denominational history. The improvisational preacher needs to be a student of his or her own church history. Read in church history about doctrinal and theological matters. It is a big matter, but there are countless stories there to be told as well.

Young people today love historical stories, the stories of real people struggling with church life and meaning. They are the stories of the church fathers, the classic lives of the early centuries. Even television channels like A&E and the History Channel work from time to time on documentary stories of early church leaders, leaders from the Reformation era, and so on. Learn and tell stories of the people who have shaped Christian doctrine and theology— such stories make for great improvisational preaching.

Some Things to Be Cautious About

In devising stories from the Bible and from church history, it is important to suggest some cautions for the young improvisational preacher. The first is that whenever you begin to study and learn a story for preaching, however you have selected it, try as much as you can to read and think about it with an open mind. That is a strange thing to say, since of course we all have open minds, and it would not occur to us *not* to read a text with an open mind. That, however, is precisely the point. We all take up a new text, a new book, a new anything, with all of the baggage of our years fully in place and ready to help us with our new task. By our natures, after the age of three or four, our minds are not very open. They are filled with a hundred or more different sets of blinders, some more powerful than others, but all of them more than make up for the work they are supposed to do—the work of keeping us on the track of our training.

So what we have been taught, and how we have been conditioned by home socializing, public or private schooling, church teaching, by early professional exposures, and on and on, we become fully and pretty near implacably conditioned to how we hear, read, or think about things. We all know this, of course, even though we are all tempted to impute it to others while we proclaim ourselves relatively free of this problem. Not so, when we are honest.

The remedy (following an admission that we, too, are undoubtedly that way) is an act of will. It is in directing ourselves to step outside of ourselves for a time—and, remarkably, we seem to be able to do just that, at least for short periods of time. One says to oneself: I am going to read this story—or this text—naively (as scholars have called it), meaning that I am going to read it as though for the first time; and I will read it as though I have only now learned to read. I will savor the words and the phrases, mulling over the sounds as I speak them aloud. Then I will ask the kinds of questions about what I have just read that I would imagine a second grader just learning to read might ask. One can, in a sense, lay aside one's conditioning—not completely mind you; we all know that. But to a significant extent it can be done, at least if one tries.

It sets up a kind of implicit introspection, a situation in which one asks, even if indirectly, what presuppositions, or assumptions, or ideas about this text I am bringing to it. Through what kinds of glasses am I reading it? Even the very act of asking that question is to set up an insightful process for discovering its answer; and with that answer, one can both consciously and deliberately read an old text in a new and potentially invigorating way. I have come to believe over many years that fresh and exciting sermons invariably result from fresh and exciting ways of reading Scripture texts and stories, even when those stories have been read by the preacher a thousand times before.

The second caution is an urging that one always pledge to be true to the text or the biblical story in one's sermon. This is one of the most violated axioms of preaching. It is not unrelated to both of the things we have just called attention to, even though, on its own, it is different. Discover what the text says; or, more accurately, to the best of your ability, discover what you truly *believe* the text to be saying; and then stick to that as you develop and preach your sermon. This is often violated in another way as well, by one who has a really good idea for preaching, and now must go looking for a text that comes pretty close to saying that idea.

Remember that people are following, or reading, the story with you, or if they aren't, they ought to be. They should have heard and followed your reading, in fact. They are depending on you to be honest about what the story says, and your task is to stay with that story, that text, and let it speak what is in it. Don't try to make the story be what you want it to be; don't even hope it will say something that is close to your thinking. Don't fudge it. That is not your job as the preacher.

The difficulty comes, of course, when we have built up particular ways of thinking and doing, whether in life, or in personal attitudes, or even in worship and service. We do it this way; we have always done it this way. I know—I have been taught well in my upbringing. But here, in this text, is it really saying something else? If I am really honest with myself, is this story going to make me look very hard at something that has been important to me? Even in matters of Christian doctrine, belief, and activity, are we finding something in a fresh, conscientious probing of a story that is forcing us to ask questions about our own ways and outlooks? That is when the matter of being true to the text really takes a potential toll; and yet some of the most remarkable moments of anyone's preaching life come when it is the preacher who is "stared down" by a story, whether it is old or new, and then has to bring that process into the pulpit with him or her.

Finally, there is one other caution. It has two parts, both of which are particularly important for contemporary preaching. It has to do with our relationship, as Christians, with those who are Jews. For the past half century, the Christian-Jewish relationship has been undergoing profound change. Increasingly, we are recognizing that we are, indeed, brothers and sisters, and we are faced with learning how to behave toward each other in that way. Many Christians, of course, believe that unless Jews become converted to Christianity they will be lost eternally; and they are more than ready to cite biblical texts to back up their understanding. Yet many Christians are also facing the fact that Christians have mistreated the Jews for too long, even through the past century; and that it is time to share love across the Christian-Jewish boundary, no matter what. And that means, as well, regardless of beliefs, that as Christians we are obligated to show respect and honor to those who value their Jewishness before the God whom they serve.

For preaching, the issue that requires caution is that we learn and work to preach in a way that does neither harm nor hurt to men, women, and young people who embrace the faith of the ancient Hebrews. Jews, including the scribes and Pharisees, do not have to be blamed year in and year out during Holy Week, even implicitly blamed, for the crucifixion of Christ. It is not necessary to preach in an overtly offensive way on texts that have Jesus calling Jewish leaders hypocrites and whitewashed sepulchers, clean outside and filthy inside. It is not necessary to celebrate the Apostle Paul's model in "forsaking" his Judaism to follow Christ. These things happened, of course, and they are a part of Christian Scripture, but different times call for different ways of handling situations; and in our time we need to preach in a way that will build bridges with those who are devout, practicing Jews. We can do that, and we can do it while being faithful to our Scriptures as well.

This is related to one other caution that, to my mind, is very important as well. It is a call to be careful about the relationship between the Old and the New Testaments. Truth be told, before the Old Testament was the Christian Old Testament, it was the Bible, the Book, Holy Scripture for the Jews. For those who are today's practicing Jews, those are still their Scriptures, aligned in a different fashion, but read in much the same way as they have been from ancient days. From a Jewish point of view, Christians "took" their Book, redid it to some extent, particularly in the ordering of its parts, so that it would say and do what we Christians needed it to say and do.

I understand well the ways in which a Christian can read the Old Testament and see the image of Christ on countless pages. So much Christian preaching will always focus on the Christology of the ancient texts; and much Christian preaching will argue, as it has since the days of the Gospels, that numerous Old Testament texts point inexorably toward Jesus of Nazareth as the Jewish Messiah; Paul more than any other early figure connected those dots. Yet given the nature of the twenty-first century world, and the role of the Jewish people and the Jewish state of Israel in it, something in us needs to learn respect not just for the Jews but for their Scriptures as well. We work, however we formulate the idea, with a borrowed book, a book that we believe points to Christ; but one, nevertheless, that thousands of practicing, faithful Jews believe that we co-opted from them. Can we preach in a way that respects that, even as we disagree with it? Occasionally, the times call for us to see ourselves and our preaching differently. My judgment is that, on this issue, we are in just such times.

CHAPTER FIVE

PREPARING THE IMPROV SERMON'S STORYBOARD

I t is only a small jump from the art of improvisation to the art of moviemaking. In fact, if there is a single defining art form of the digital age it is the cutting and intercutting, the juxtaposing and overlaying, of images and sounds—the art, in short, of making movies. Whether they are music videos for MTV and its spin-offs, the handheld shots of the Internet's garage bands, the Hollywood blockbusters *The Matrix* or *Harry Potter*, or the homemade clips put together for this Sunday's youth gathering, they are all based squarely in the century-old process of shooting and editing film. That process provides not just a metaphor for creating a spoken message for platform or pulpit; it provides a lively model for how to *prepare* today's contemporary sermon.

In short, the effective improv sermon is created the way a digital movie or video is—not surprising for preaching in a digital age to digital people. It is researched, thought through, and then broken down into a series of individual shots, or sequences, that are then edited together into the finished production, ready for delivery, or presentation.

Three things about this process, though, are particularly important. First, in this preparation process, as we saw earlier, the sermon must be handled as though it is the story. It has to be worked out and presented like a story. It will have its beginning, middle, and end; its sense of unfolding or progress; its clear understanding of what the creator would like the outcome to be. There may well be shorter stories—as we saw in an earlier chapter—within the larger story, but, like a movie, the overall structure of the piece is designed as a story.

Second, the movie model for the sermon is more like a documentary than a feature film. That is, the pieces are real and have substance, with each one contributing to what is said. It is to be a passionate telling, of course; but, like a great documentary, it is about real life and real things about life. For example, not long ago the great racehorse from the 1930s named Seabiscuit made a comeback as both a feature film and a documentary, both based on a best-selling book. Each of the films tells the Seabiscuit story, but they tell it in strikingly different ways. The feature film does so by constructing countless details, even making them up as need be. It has a fanciful, overly dramatic feel to it, playing to the hilt on the story's emotions. The documentary, on the other hand, is spare and sparse, letting the materials speak for themselves. It tells the story from beginning to end, and with great natural drama. As a result, the sense of reality, even truth, comes through the story much more directly and profoundly. One need only see both versions to appreciate the difference. It is the difference between watching something done by actors and something that is utterly authentic. One is not watching a horse *like* Seabiscuit, but one is actually *seeing* Seabiscuit run in the documentary.

The third thing of importance is that both the feature film and the documentary are prepared in essentially the same way. Each is carefully storyboarded, the movie process by which all basic planning and preparation are done. It is not unusual today, for example, when one purchases a DVD version of a prominent movie to receive in the package some pages of the film's storyboard. A storyboard is a set of cartoon-like panels in which designers create drawings indicating how scenes should look, what they should contain, the viewpoint of the camera, and how they should change from shot to shot and scene to scene. The storyboard is the well-developed skeleton from which the movie actually emerges.

Preparation of the improv sermon can best be understood as the making of a storyboard. The storyboard will play the same role in the sermon as it does for the documentary film. It will be the guide, or the plan, from which the completed sermon's overall story will emerge. In the typical sermon of about twenty-five minutes— which, with improv preaching, is a very good length—no fewer than eight to ten story panels will be required. Each panel will represent—or contain—one sequence, and they will be arranged in order. Understanding the sequences as shots on the storyboard will also make the overall sermon very easy to memorize for speaking without manuscript or notes. In the speaking, each panel will ideally take about three to five minutes. Each will make its own well-defined contribution to the overall movement of what the preacher wants to say. Not only is a sermon prepared as a storyboard easy to *memorize*, but also, by its storylike nature, it is very *memorable* as well.

Before discussing the storyboard process for the message in detail, though, it is important to say one thing as emphatically as possible. It is this: *Preach your own sermons.* It should really be said again: Just as you should find, develop, and tell your own personal stories, you should also create and prepare your own sermons. If you do, the sermon will actually *sound* like it has come from you and you only. In this age of the Internet, the lifting and using—whether buying, borrowing, or, more commonly, stealing—of someone else's sermon has become one of the most serious problems confronting the church and its preachers. Preachers used to be able to find the sermons of other preachers only in books; now, countless Web sites exist *only* to sell or otherwise make sermon outlines and manuscripts available to whomever wants them. So when Saturday night rolls around and the preacher has not yet gotten to sermon preparation, the easiest thing in the world is to go to a sermon Web site, download an outline, look it over, and use it for preaching the next morning. Tragically, for some preachers, the day of having to prepare their own sermons, even for contemporary worship, is over.

What many preachers do not realize, though, is that congregants can always tell when this is the case. It shows in countless subtle but telltale ways. The preacher, for example, despite using only notes, is conspicuously tied to the paper in front of him or her. Moreover, the preacher gets lost easily, not knowing well the track that his or her borrowed outline has laid down. The preacher, in short, who seems vaguely but noticeably disconnected, not sure exactly what to say, and working mostly with clichéd language.

All told, the most serious problem with preaching from someone else's sermon outline or manuscript is that the preacher, whatever else he or she is doing, is not speaking from the heart—*the one thing that preaching improvisationally is intentionally designed to make happen.* Today's contemporary worshippers really do want to *see* and *feel* and *experience* the preacher's heart: that is the very essence of creating that experience of God that has concerned us throughout this book.

There is only one way to preach from your heart, and that is to work throughout the week, as moments present themselves, on devising and developing *your own sermons.* That sermon, then, becomes a part of you as you live with it in the days leading up to worship; it grows in you and on you, and when you preach it—it *will* be yours, your own stories, your own stories from the Bible, your own thinking and feeling, your own testimony to the faith in Christ that is in you. With that, no matter what the subject or how you improvisationally get it said, your congregants will bless you and praise God for the gift of the Christian message that has been given to them.

There are, of course, many ways to prepare a sermon, and no lack of books to explain them all. What effective, time-saving preparation boils down to, though—particularly for improvisational preaching—is that you need to develop a *routine* of your own—a systematic, repetitive process for creating your sermon, your message. Because of the pressures of time, this routine should be one that you can depend on week by week, one that will not let you down; it should be a procedure, at the same time, that will enable you to keep your sermons fresh, varied, and powerful every time you move to the platform or pulpit.

Is there only one way to prepare a sermon, one that works well for all of the sermons that one preaches? The answer is *yes*—as surprising as that may sound to a lot of preachers and homileticians. Look at it, though, through the eyes of a good filmmaker. The filmmaker learns the basics of making movies. Even though the technology may change from time to time, and there will occasionally be new things to pick up, there is *still* only one way to make a movie. The filmmaker devises a plan, then a script and storyboard; after that, he or she takes the camera and, following the plan, shoots the shots called for in the plan. The shots, or scenes, or sequences, are collected as bits and pieces. The filmmaker then edits the pieces together, again following the storyboard, into the completed film.

That's the moviemaking process. When one has mastered it, one can make *any kind of movie one wishes*—a comedy or tragedy, sci-fi or horror, something tasteful or tasteless. The fundamentals are the same. Even if one goes from Hollywood to independent, from feature to documentary, once the basics of moviemaking become second nature, then the filmmaker's own unique sense of fun, insight, and outlook kicks in.

The very same thing is true for public speaking—and for the sermon. Like the movie, whatever kind it is, the sermon starts with an idea. "I want to make a movie about . . ."; or "I want to preach a sermon about . . . ," and the blank is filled in. That idea can come from anyplace—from something one has often thought about, or someone has asked about, or, as with much preaching, some particular text of the Bible. Sometimes the preacher will have no choice but to use a prescribed text, like the lectionary text for the day. It is not unusual, either, for the preacher to be free to select any text that he or she wants for a given sermon.

Next, like making a movie, the idea for the sermon, whether drawn from a biblical text or someplace else, is translated into a clear statement, meaning an overt notion of "here is what I would like to *say* about this topic or this theme." "I would like for everyone to come out of the sermon knowing . . ." and then the sentence is completed. Or, "I would like for the people who share my sermon to experience . . ." and then indicate what that is. While this process may be somewhat vague at this point, practice makes one quite good at it; and doing it is important to give the sermon its initial sense of direction; its kick-start, in a sense. Often, once your topic is in hand, this step is a statement of what you really believe about the topic you want your sermon to convey. Even though the work of study and planning is still ahead of us, now we have a direction, one that will indeed take us down the path ahead.

Next comes the selection of a biblical text, if that has not been done in identifying the sermon's topic or theme. In most cases this will be a single text, though it is not uncommon for the sermon to be built around a central text while making use of other supportive texts. Topic and text now need to inform each other. This means that the preacher must study the text carefully and correctly. There are numerous books and guides for textual and background study, and this is not the place for us to pursue how this is done. But, as we indicated in our chapter on the need for preaching the Bible, it is absolutely essential for the contemporary preacher to bring to the sermon the full impact of Holy Scripture, regardless of the topic or theme.

As you study the text—something to which no fewer than two hours should be devoted for each sermon—take notes, lots of notes. These can be notes about your observations as you study, things that strike you as important in your reading and meditation, notes about the text's background and origins, notes about the text's uniqueness, even notes about how others have handled it in their commentaries and Bible helps. Your notes may well become part of the sermon itself, often in ways that you do not expect or cannot anticipate during your study. What you learn from your study of text is exactly what your hearers may need to learn as well. What you learn in your study of text is often what you should teach in your sermon. In many ways, few things are more important to giving a contemporary sermon life and memorability than what the speaker *teaches* about a particular text, biblical passage, situation, or character.

You should now have a set of biblical notes and materials as a groundwork. If this is so, it is time for some serious personal brainstorming. The question now is what other materials, outside of the biblical framework, can illuminate the topic or theme, as well as the text, about which you will preach. Good material collected here will result in a very good movie-style sermon; thin or poor material, or even a lack of material collected at this point, will show itself in a weak or thin movielike sermon.

What is the contemporary preacher, like the moviemaker, collecting at this brainstorming stage? One tries, as we indicated earlier, to find stories of one's own that relate to the idea or topic of the sermon. If one has kept a file of stories, now is the time to go through them. If not, one rehearses events and traumas of the past week or two to try to discover a related matter that can be turned into a good story—like the story of Dr. Nathan and Myra. When a story is found, or devised anew from experience, it is sketched out in one's notes for what will become a scene or sequence in the sermon.

One hunts for other story materials in the Bible itself—there are countless valuable, usable stories, many of them in the Old Testament, that throw light on ideas or topics for sermons. These are stories like Barzillai's. Often the preacher can remember a story once heard or read that is called to mind by this topic; then it becomes a matter of hunting it down. Invariably this hunt is worth the effort, though it may, indeed, take some time to locate it and get it right. The preacher should be warned, however, not to try to tell a story that is only *vaguely* remembered. Invariably, there will be people present who know the biblical material fairly well, and will be more than ready to correct the preacher's errors. When you remember a story, find it, read it anew, study it, and tell it vividly.

Often, one knows some history that bears on a particular sermon idea, and a quick trip to the public library will pay off with a vivid, insightful addition to the sermon's topic or theme. Or one knows something from contemporary media or popular culture—a television ad or a situation comedy, such as an episode of *Friends* or *Seinfeld*, or something like that. Notes need to be taken so that the brainstorming will pay off. For now, let your list grow without worrying about what, if anything, you will do with these materials. Sometimes an event of some prominence in your community will come to mind from the sermon's idea or theme; and it, too, should be checked for accuracy if you make notes about it.

One other thing: in this brainstorming, or this collecting of information, it is not unusual to encounter ideas about what the Christian should do concerning the idea or topic, or even text. Here, too, such ideas should never pass without notes being made to oneself. Ideas, even good ones, are often ephemeral—and often they will not be easily called back to mind, even just two or three days later during sermon development. Experienced preachers, writers, and filmmakers all know that when a good idea enters the head, even if it is the middle of the night, it is dangerous to wait till morning to make a note of it. Often it is gone with the daylight. Get up and write it down, and it will be waiting in the morning, safely within your grasp.

Once this information gathering is done—and it can be anywhere from a one- to two-day process, scattered amid numerous other tasks—it is time to go through the sifting process. This is the creation of an organizational scheme for all of the ideas, stories, and materials that have now been collected. Here again, guidance for the task will come from the filmmaker. How does the maker of a short film work from an assortment of notes and ideas now listed in random order but all held together by a common idea or topic or theme? It is not a difficult question to answer; and even though different filmmaker might use different methods or even different schemes of work, their fundamental process is the same since they are all working with the same unique medium.

This is where the filmmaker's all-important storyboard comes into play—and the urging of this chapter is that the contemporary preacher can do no better than to adapt the filmmaker's storyboard to the creative fashioning of the sermon. It provides, as my students have amply demonstrated, a surprisingly simple and efficient *visual* way to both prepare and present the sermon. For purposes of simplicity and smoothness of work, an eight-panel storyboard works best. If the preacher occasionally needs an extra panel or two, or even one or two fewer, which is less common, the storyboard process is still the key to unity, variety, and clarity for the improv sermon. Each panel of the storyboard is a box, with the eight panels set up like this:

1.	2.	3.	4.
———	———	———	———
5.	6.	7.	8.
———	———	———	———

The major difference between the film's storyboard and the improv sermon's storyboard is that the film's will contain sketches and drawings, often along with some notes, while the sermon's storyboard will contain notes only. We will not draw actual pictures in our panels (though some may like the idea and try it); instead, we are going to write ourselves the kinds of notes in each one that will result in verbal pictures and messages when we preach our sermon. The sermon storyboard gives us a handy and remarkably easy way to see the development from scene to scene of our sermon. Each panel will provide us with the next sequence in the progression of how we will tell our sermon's story.

Notice that each panel is divided into a larger top section and a smaller lower one. Now we are ready to comb through all of our sermon preparation notes, materials from our work in biblical texts as well as materials that we have added from our brainstorming about current issues and situations. We are looking (in the case of our eight panels) for eight separate scenes or pieces from what we have collected. Usually, more than eight will take us too long to talk through in our sermon; fewer than eight will tend not to be enough. In most cases since we will talk through each panel in three or four minutes, the result gives us the length of sermon that works about right for almost all occasions.

We now make selections in order to fill in each panel—in the larger upper section of each—with a brief summary, a very short paragraph, of the particular material for that scene or sequence, that panel. The rule is simple: no more than one item for each panel. A panel may be illustrative (i.e., the Dr. Nathan story is one panel). It may be the explanation of a word or concept; it may be a particular section of notes about the text or texts. It may even be a brief part of the preacher's own testimony. But one item per panel, or the process will not work. The idea is that each panel will then make its own contribution to the progression of the sermon's story from beginning, through development, to end. For example, what will be in the panel that ends the sermon? What kind of material?

114

The first panel should contain how the sermon is introduced; and so on. The brief paragraph is then written into the *top section* of each panel. It should be full enough (whether handwritten or inserted by computer) so that one knows clearly and completely what it involves. In this way, when all of the panels are filled, one can readily move through them all to get a sense of the continuity and drama of how the sermon—like a movie—unfolds.

For purposes of good sermon-making, just as for good filmmaking, it is important to go over, often again and again, the movement from panel to panel to see if they need to be rearranged, or if something is missing, or if, as sometimes happens, they just don't quite work in this particular order. Remember that what you are creating with the panels is the *form* of a story. It is not the form of an essay, or a term paper, or even an argument or debate. It is the form of a story.

The set up, for the sermon as for the movie, is a laying out of individual pieces. Often this process will not be clear at all to the hearer—in fact, one almost hopes that it will not be visible or detectable. This is the way interest is built within an audience. An Alfred Hitchcock movie, for example, can go on for twenty or more minutes with locations developed, with characters being introduced and moved about—clearly with something *about* to happen—but the viewer can only hold everything in suspense, since nothing in those opening minutes will make sense. One knows, however, that in time they will—and the suspense is what the moviemaker wants. This is the setup, and it is a remarkably important part of the movie—as well as the good improv message.

It is in the middle of the movie that the story is developed, where the audience is is not only fully drawn in but immersed. Some issue emerges for those participating in what is happening. Some problem is encountered that must be worked through. Some dilemma is raised that poses a threat. The story develops, scene by scene. This is what the improv sermon seeks to do as well. It moves like a story to be solved in some fashion. The plot thickens; and even in thinking about an improv sermon, as the scenes or sequences are set in place, each one should move the plot or the idea or the problem along.

Finally, everything must work itself out in some satisfying way. We are going to refer to it as an ending, rather than as a climax because often the ending is much lower key. It can often be quieter than such words imply—and still be a very good, satisfying wrap-up.

So how do we arrange the scenes or sequences of the improv sermon to reflect this story-driven dynamic? Like making a movie, this, too, is a process of careful editing. Editing is an arranging of shots, placing one right after the other. As in good storytelling, each panel should elicit an unspoken response of "Yes, yes, go on—then what happened?" With the making of an improv sermon, it will not necessarily be that clean-cut, but that is exactly the dynamic of improvisation itself, as we saw in our earlier discussion. It is the way of the story.

So—what are some guidelines for creating the storyboard for the improv sermon?

My experience has been that various combinations can work, depending on the materials collected. The normal arrangements would be what we could call 2-3-3, or 3-2-3, or 3-3-2. By those numbers we mean that there could be 2 or 3 panel sequences in the setup section, as many as 2, 3, or even 4 panels in the progress or middle section, and the 2 or 3 panels for the ending section. I have found in working with students on this kind of sermon that the best conceptualization of the work is to follow these three parts of the story process, allocating a given number of sequences to flesh out each of those story-oriented parts. It needs to be kept in mind, though, that this is merely a scaffolding for creating the sermon's structure—these three parts will disappear and only the eight sequences or panels will be visible when the sermon is preached.

There is no way for anyone to dictate to the moviemaker, or the preacher, the order in which the scenes are to be arranged on the storyboard to produce the final result. In fact, probably more than at any other stage in the process, *here* is where the creator's own personality and genius take over. Here is where the creation carries its maker's unique stamp. Nothing in your arrangement of sequences should be easily predictable to an audience member, a congregant. Try for as much suspense as your arrangement will allow, being absolutely quirky, if necessary, in what you do. Think of creating a story with your scenes or sequences, and then, in your delivery, you will end up telling the storyboard's panels one after the other, just as you would tell a good story.

Some say that if you set up a problem early on in the sermon, you can use the progression of how to solve the problem as a means of suspense building. To an extent that is true, but many good sermon ideas or topics are not about problems as such; and the task is simply to build sequences that turn over the preacher's cards one by one, without revealing the last card in the hand, the card that will win the game. My experience has been that when students of preaching consciously work at setting up sequences that gradually tell the story—and tell it piece by piece—even without a deliberate problem set up at the outset, they create sermons filled with lively, creative, satisfying suspense, which translates into keen audience interest in what one is saying.

This brings us to the *other* guideline for both creating and evaluating one's alignment of scenes or sequences for the improv sermon. It has to do with the fact that a sermon—particularly an improvisational, entertaining one—*must have something to say*, something that is worth saying because it arises from biblical authority. Earlier, we indicated that most often the improvisational preacher will know what that is at the time of the selection of topic or theme or even biblical text. This is often the motivating guide for the materials one looks for and eventually chooses for the sermon's storyboard.

Two things, though, need to be kept in mind. First, sometimes that idea of what one wants to say, as clear as it might be at the beginning, undergoes change in the process of study, reflection, and research; in fact, this is not uncommon at all. The point is that the good improv preacher will stay constantly open to that possibility. It should not be a fearful thing, though undoubtedly it is for some people. What it represents, though, is growth—the kind of growth that study, learning, reflection, and meditation invariably produce. The preacher should also be aware that *when* such change or growth, however subtle, takes place within the preacher's mind and heart, that changing should find its way into the actual content of the sermon itself. The second thing that is important about what one wants to say in the sermon is that once the storyboard is formed, the preacher should evaluate it carefully to determine if one overall idea, whatever that is, actually gets said in a clear, convincing fashion. This, too, is why the storyboard approach works so well: it provides a highly sensitive way of taking stock concerning the plan for the sermon's outcome.

Now the sermon's storyboard becomes a very living piece of work. Now, just as the moviemaker can study the storyboard panel by panel and literally see the movie's setup, development, and outcome, so the preacher can with his or her own improv sermon. It is at this point that weak panels need to be changed, or panels that now are out of order can be realigned, or panels that are extraneous can be dropped. The sermon can actually be visualized in this form.

Now we have written our short summary of that particular scene into the top section of each panel. Now we can read through each one and across the panels to follow the sermon's development. There is one other crucial step, though, in finishing the storyboard. As you saw in the previous diagram, each panel was divided into a large top section and a smaller lower one. The last step takes us to the panels one more time—this time to the lower section of each one, the part below the broken line. That lower section now is to be filled in. Read each panel's summary and then, below the broken line, write a four- or five-word summary of what is above the broken line. This is to be the memory line for each panel. To learn these lower lines, in order, is to be able to recreate the entire storyboard panel by panel—in an improvisational fashion. It all works—and becomes an extremely useful way of learning to both prepare and preach the creative, improv sermon.

We need to stop here, though, so that we can illustrate and demonstrate this entire storyboard process by creating a sermon of our own from beginning to end. This sermon was planned as part of a series I preached on the lesser—though no less important—characters of the Bible. They are not main characters about whom we preach often, but those named people who show up in their movielike supporting roles. Named people, however. My view is that since we common people tend to stand, in a real sense, where *they* are, we can sometimes learn more about Christ and our own Christian faith from them than from the great heroes of Scripture, as important as they are. Quite high on my list of intriguing supporting characters is the young man in the New Testament named Demas. He is not well known, and even less spoken of today, probably because of what he did. In one sense, he is the idea or the topic for the sermon. Even though I have read a number of times the three texts where his name appears, I am still not sure how the sermon will be developed. In another sense, this sermon is about Christian betrayal or rejection; it is the negative side of the Christian coin.

For me, this is a very important sermon for young people, particularly young adults, twenty- and thirty-somethings, since Demas was one of them. Young people need to know about Demas; they need to learn of him and from him. This is not to say that Demas is not relevant to older adults, too—but Demas's story is a story of youth and temptations unique to it.

Two of Demas's appearances in the New Testament are with Paul, Luke, and a couple of others; he is mentioned in Paul's letters. He is mentioned in Colossians 4:14 and in Philemon verse 24. While those texts will be utilized in the sermon—they have to be—the most significant text in which Demas appears is 2 Timothy 4:10; it comes immediately after that heart-wrenching text from Paul about his being poured out as a drink offering, since the time for his departure is at hand. He has, he says, fought the good fight, finished the race, kept the faith; as a result, prepared and waiting for him is the "crown of righteousness" that shall be given to all those who have loved Christ's appearing.

Then Paul urges Timothy to come to him quickly—since, he says powerfully in verse 10, "Demas, in love with this present world, has deserted me and gone to Thessalonica." That line, like an iceberg, so small on the surface of what it says, yet beneath its surface is a gigantic boulder of emotion, frustration, even heartbreak. You can actually hear that in the way Paul phrases the line; he has to get it out but not dwell on it. Move on, move on. Paul has entered his own life-threatening crisis, and he cannot be distracted. In fact, he is trying very hard not to be distracted, particularly by a deserting colleague.

With that, the first phase of my sermon preparation is underway. I first try to look as closely as possible at this text and its context. To deal with the text, though, is hunting in a craggy, dark cave. What can we say about Demas? Obviously not very much, except that we can pick up some clues here and there, acknowledging that we are in Sherlock Holmes territory, except that, in our case, we know that we may not be able to solve the crime. There is, however, a place here for what old preachers when I was growing up liked to call the "sanctified imagination."

My reflection on all three of these texts and their surroundings leads me to three things—first to the nature of the group that Paul attracted to himself. How nice if we could know more about who they were and how he did that. He met the young Timothy on one of his mission trips; we can only assume that that was probably true of the others. What we have scattered throughout Paul's writings are *names*, often names that appear multiple times, almost always with affectionate references attached to them. Timothy is best known, and Titus—who was he? How many can we identify, or know anything about? I have written about John

Mark elsewhere; but there is Crescens, Epaphras, and at the end of 2 Timothy we meet Erastus, Trophimus, Eubulus, Pudens, Linus, Claudia—yes, there were young women in the circle around Paul as well.

Paul was well known after so many years on the road, since he was someone who had not only preached, but also had written extensively. He was in demand. Moreover, he had a charisma that caught the attention of bright young people, and he taught them the gospel, trying deliberately and diligently—you can tell—to groom them to take up the roles in ministry that near the end of his life were everywhere. What an incredible experience it must have been to be counted among Paul's disciples! Challenging, absolutely engaging, dangerous, an intellectual feast—to have the great apostle refer to you in one of his letters to a new church—absolutely a chance of a lifetime for a young, ambitious Christian who catches the fire of Paul's gospel!

Demas was one of them, probably with all of those promising characteristics; Paul includes him in his greetings list not in one letter, but in *two*—one of them being among his most intimate letters, to Philemon. Each of the three times that Paul refers to Demas, Luke's name is very close by. This leads to the second clue that, in my judgment, may not be insignificant: that Demas was brought into Paul's circle by Luke, the physician who seems to have devoted most of the latter years of his life to Paul. Is it possible that Demas was a medical person, too, someone that Luke was acquainted with from earlier times and kept in touch with? While we have no way to know this for sure, it does appear that Demas was with Paul and Luke for quite a while, long enough at any rate for there to have been a bonding among the three of them, and possibly with Timothy, since Paul pointedly informs Timothy of the desertion.

The second part of the text that particularly registers with me is that basic element from Paul's phrase about Demas: he left because he has loved the present world or the present age. As opposed to what? The age to come? The spirit age? However we end up stating it, we can infer here a reference that we know from numerous of Paul's other writings—that there is this world, the material, sinful one, and the other world, the world of the Spirit, the world into which Christ bids us enter. The comment about Demas brings both of those worlds into sharp relief.

The third thing I end up puzzling over from the text is that when Paul says that Demas has loved this world, he uses the Greek term *agape*, which is that special word usually reserved for divine love; Paul does not use *phileo*, calling Demas a "friend of the world," or even *eros*, the word that could imply a physical, visceral attachment to it. No, it is agape. Why, though—why—did he use that word, and what does that word, placed here, suggest? I do not have an answer, but the question is more than intriguing to me. I am not even sure, though, that I will deal with this in my sermon.

At any rate, those are most of my study notes on the texts about Demas. There is no way, I understand, to say why Demas left Paul, except to use Paul's remarkable language. What that phrase involves, however, will become a crucial part of a sermon to be preached here. Moreover, my mind is stretching: I may want to talk about avoiding the Demas syndrome, or something like that. My sermon is underway, and it is time for me to search for other materials outside of the texts that will give my sermon substance and relevance. I have to confess that, initially, that is very difficult for me to do, though I do not plan to spend too much time on this particular item. There is no way that I cannot make a note of it, however, since it forms a kind of testimony, something that I take to be a legitimate part of any good sermon—if it is not overdone.

The fact is that I find myself attracted to Demas because during a significant stretch of my middle life, I *was* Demas; I actually know him fairly well, much better than I find it comfortable to admit. I know him because I know myself during those years. I grew up in the church, spent my early years in ministry, then moved over into higher education, and at some point deserted the church and my own faith. I can look back and see what kinds of things pulled me away; and they were not so much sinful things as they were things that choked out what used to be important to me—no, many of those things were plainly sinful. Ironically, I did love—really love, agapelike—those "things of this world" that took over where I was and what I was. The point is that the Demas syndrome is not unknown or even unusual today. It is a serious threat to the life of every young to middle-aged Christian. How much I want to say about that in my sermon I don't know yet; but this is not a difficult connection to make for myself or even others I know and have known.

I do think often, too, about how I managed to come back to the church. It took some profound help from some dedicated friends; and it took a whole new commitment on my part to Christ, to church, and to Christian disciplines. There are things in *that* part of my own story that also enable me to connect the Demas saga to today, but, again, I will have to be cautious about how far I carry it. I am very aware, though, that this sermon will probably be different from many that I normally prepare and preach improvisationally. But these kinds of sermons cannot be ignored when the Holy Spirit seems to be leading the preacher.

There will be other things, other notes from my brainstorming, but these are enough items to make clear the process. So I am ready to work on my sermon sequences using a blank storyboard. Some of my sequences are ready to fall into place fairly well, but not all of them. With material like this, it is always better in my judgment to start with textual things, which I will do. As my research and reflection about Demas has progressed, as I have already indicated from my notes on Demas, I have gotten a sense of *how* to start and how to break things up. It is the latter panels that are still a bit up in the air. Nevertheless, even as I start to think my way sequentially through what I have in front of me, even those concluding pieces will become clearer, I know.

Here, then, is my storyboard's growing arrangement, with the eight panels that I now, for purposes of brevity, can fill in—for now the summary top sections of each panel.

1. Paul, the charismatic leader, attracts around him a remarkable group of young men and women. Who are they? Identify some— some well known, some not very well known. The lists are scattered throughout his letters. What a thrill (and danger) it must have been to have been with him.	2. One of those was the man named Demas. Where do we find out about Demas? Look at the warm words about him written by Paul. Look who Demas actually knew— including Philemon. And Demas seems to have known Luke fairly well. Could he have been recruited by Luke?	3. But there is a text in Timothy that tells us what happened to Demas; or what Demas did. He is the saddest of Paul's associates. What happened to him—we read the text and still are not sure whether we know or not. Demas has "deserted me . . ."	4. Ironically, I know Demas. I do. I understand him. Tell my story of being faithful, of following, and then, because of this world, leaving. My dad knew I was like Demas. He preached a sermon about Demas and, without naming me, he named me. I can see, at least somewhat, into Demas's heart.
The group that Paul attracted.	Who was this Demas?	Demas forsakes Paul.	Demas's story is my story.
5. What are the two worlds of the Demas story? Demas loved this world more than he loved the other one. Material or physical? Heavenly or sinful? What is Paul's way of talking about these two worlds? Do we all have to choose? It appears we do.	6. What causes us to fall into the Demas trap, the Demas syndrome? What causes us to give up something we have made a commitment to— and turn back to where we came from? What was pulling on Demas? We are guessing, of course; but our guesses are worth making.	7. So we have to choose—choices are not just a part of life; they are part of Christian life. Choose life. Choose to be faithful. Or choose to turn away. Choose to return to the world. How did Demas choose? What can we say about him?	8. What are the outcomes of our choosing? What does Paul say, or imply, about Demas's choice—he has not just chosen to leave; he has chosen the path down. If we follow Paul, and Christ, we choose—Paul's great language about the "crown of righteousness" (2 Timothy 4:8). To choose is a serious matter.
Paul's two worlds— what?	Why Demas's decision?	We have to choose, too.	Choose the crown of righteousness.

The sermon now has a story quality about it, even a crescendo effect that I like, ending on a strongly positive note. I also think it has a strong sense of testimony to it, both Demas's and mine, if I may say it that way. The sermon sounds negative on one hand—and indeed it is intended to sound that way. It is also intended, panel by panel, to probe into the psyche and the soul of this obscure but very important young man. Because the sermon is edited onto my storyboard and presented piece by piece, it has an unfolding quality to it. Despite using my own story, my own testimony, it will be brief and not graphic—intended only to connect someone in the present to Paul's day. The sermon will remain about Demas. And although the sermon is about Demas, it is not about him at all in the end. It is about Paul, the one who said "be imitators of me, as I am of Christ" (1 Cor 11:1). It is a sermon about Christ, and the choices that we are called to make ultimately about him. The end is positive, upbeat—as moving a call to make a choice for Christ as I am able to make. It will be a biblically based statement calling people, particularly young people, to be committed to a holy, Spirit-filled life. When this is presented improvisationally, from my storyboard and memorized sequences, I think it will have exactly the kind of pull that I would like to achieve with it. I will title it, "The Demas Syndrome."

Improvisational sermons are wonderful to listen to. Anyone can learn to prepare them following these storyboard steps. Storyboarding is at the heart of the preparation process. It is clean, easy to grasp and learn—and, for the hearers, very easy to follow. Don't make things too complicated. The storyboard helps you keep the outline simple and memorable. But don't dumb things down either. Good study and imaginative sequences lead to original and fun sermon storyboards. The process works. If you learn it, practice it, and make it your own, your sermons will glisten with freshness, vigor, and inspiration. No one—no one—will go away unaffected by hearing your speaking of the gospel of Christ.

Epilogue

As every generation does, this generation of contemporary preachers and those who follow it will produce some great preachers. Some can already be seen on the horizon. Others, now in training, will come along rapidly, taking their place in still-growing churches. Still others, now growing up their churches, will catch the spirit and fire for preaching the gospel in coming years. In all of its forms and models, what we now know as contemporary worship is clearly the church of the twenty-first century. It will most likely change the world of this new century in ways far more positive and far-reaching than the Christian church in recent decades has been able to do.

Whether that actually becomes true or not, however, may depend more than anything else on the preaching that takes place in a million or more different Christian pulpits and platforms in coming days. If the preaching is set aside, or is relegated to a secondary place within the dynamic services of music and media, then the future of the Christian gospel may well fall into jeopardy. Whatever else happens, no church can do without at least one single, flesh-and-blood voice that stands in its midst week after week speaking out in countless ways: "I am not ashamed of the gospel of Christ, for it is the power of salvation to everyone who believes."

That must not be lost in contemporary worship, though the danger of that happening is very real.

The gospel must be spoken openly, dynamically, and with emphasis. It must be told in stories, real stories—from the Scriptures and from real life. It must be told with passion and emotion, with intelligence and creativity. It must be told with energy, always energy and intensity. In one of those interviews with young Christians from the Lilly study we referred to at the beginning, Albert, another church member, was asked: "If you had one or two things you could tell preachers that would help energize you when you were listening to a sermon, what would that be?"

> The preacher . . . can't just stand at the podium and flip papers and read. I want to know personal stories. I want to know stories from the Bible. . . . You just can't read to me and send me home. I want to feel it. Folks want to do that. . . . The young folks of my age group, . . . they're saying the same thing. That's why their brothers and sisters don't come because they don't get nothing out of it.[1]

We know very well that even young people, young adults, when they decide to make church a part of their lives (as countless do these days), they engage in what old-timers used to call "church shopping"; it is the process of visiting first this church and then that one—looking for the place that feels right, a place that in a sense calls to them. We also know that what is usually most attractive to these searching young adults—as strange as it is to say—is not the music, or even the liturgy; it is not even the quality of child care or ease of parking. Invariably, it is the preacher—how the preacher appears, what the preacher says, and, most importantly, *how* the preacher says it. Read the Lilly interview segments again—or find and read the interviews themselves. You will see that that is the case.

Apart from everything we have said in these pages, though, about how contemporary sermons are made or what they are made from, two things come together in the preacher to actually create the setting of the sermon—that give the sermon its ultimate power in the church. Two spirits are always at work together—the Holy Spirit and the human spirit of the preacher.

Every person who preaches, whether evangelical, mainline Protestant, Orthodox, or Roman Catholic, knows that preaching is a holy activity, one that we cannot do as we should without the presence of the Spirit of God within and behind our work. Theologies of how the Holy Spirit works in the sermon when we preach vary widely, to be sure; but no one who takes to pulpit or platform does so without a consciousness of God energizing the work. If the Holy Spirit is not in the sermon, it may be a speech, but it will not be a sermon.

A book like this one, however, that concentrates on and explores the public speaking nature of the preaching event is often criticized for sounding like the process is all human and not divine. The fact is that what makes preaching the gospel so very complex is that it is not just a speech, but a divine, Holy Spirit-breathed speech. It is not one or the other, holy or human; it is, in truth, a both/and event. So how are we to understand this unique form of public address, the improvisational sermon?

I have thought much about this dilemma, and have come to the conclusion that if we go back more than a hundred years, to a preacher still well known for his grasp of the nature of the sermon, we will find some of the best help with this matter that we could ask for—and it is fitting for us to do so as we end a little book on the *future* of preaching.

In 1877, one of the great preachers of his era—Phillips Brooks of Boston—delivered what were, and still are, known as the Lyman Beecher Lectures on Preaching at the Divinity School of then Yale College. But it was Brooks's lectures, delivered when the lectureship was no more than a couple of years old, that stand to this day as among the best ever. They are still in print, and still worth the time of any preacher, even today's young contemporary preacher.

In his lectures, Brooks provided one of the truly lasting definitions of preaching, famous as much for its brevity as for its insight. He defined preaching as the presentation of "truth through personality." Here is the way he said it, though today his masculine language would undoubtedly take cognizance of the powerful role of women who preach. Brooks said:

> [Preaching] has in it two essential elements, truth and personality. Neither of those can it spare and still be preaching. The truest truth, the most authoritative statement of God's will, communicated in any other way then through the personality of brother man to men is not preached truth. Suppose it written on the sky, suppose it embodied in a book which has been so long held in reverence as the direct utterance of God that the vivid personality of the men who wrote its pages was well-nigh faded out of it; in neither of these cases is there any preaching. And on the other hand, if men speak to other men that which they do not claim for truth, if they use their powers of persuasion or of entertainment to make other men listen to their speculations, or do their will, or applaud their cleverness, that is not preaching either. The first lacks personality. The second lacks truth. And preaching is the bringing of truth through personality. It must have both elements.[2]

Brooks's explanation has truly stood the test of time. It is in preaching, Brooks said, in that remarkable moment when the preacher stands before people on platform or in pulpit, it is there, literally, that two great God-created spirits come together. It is there that they meet in one of the most important and sacred events in all Christian experience. It is there that what we might call the human spirit and what we know as the Holy Spirit intersect. It is not that they become fused with each other—not in any way should it become confused with that. It is, however, the place in which human spirit and Holy Spirit become allies with each other.

Theologians, to say nothing of preachers, know very well how difficult it is to draw up a well-rounded theology of the Holy Spirit;

few things in the Bible, both Old and New Testaments, are more elusive than the ever shifting, constantly moving Spirit of God; and theologizing about it, however helpful, does little to pin it down in the long run. We can pick a hundred texts from here and there where the Spirit is talked about, we can make notes and then try to sort though them, hoping to understand what the Holy Spirit is and how it does its day-to-day work in the church and in our lives. For example, we can take the gospel writer John's idea in chapter 14 that the Holy Spirit is for us a comforter, the Greek word *paraclete*—"I will send the paraclete," Jesus says. The word itself means "one who stands alongside you." In our thinking about the role of the Holy Spirit in preaching, that is probably the best sense of it on which we can draw.

It is a theological mistake, however, to assume that in the pulpit the preacher's words somehow turn into God's words—that when you hear the preacher talking it is God who is actually talking. Of course miracles can happen, but nothing that I can find in Scripture suggests that when the preacher stands before people a miracle turns his or her words into God's words; and yet that has become a dominant theology of preaching over the past century. We can probably say that the Holy Spirit in some way infuses biblical texts—we do believe in the inspiration of Scripture, despite wide differences in understanding what that means—but there is little evidence that that inspiration extends to a preacher's feeble attempts to explain or expound upon those texts.

On the other hand, it will not do to say that the preacher is just a person who talks at a given time and place about some religious subject. The preacher is much more than that; on that, biblical texts are very clear. The preacher is a person set aside for holy work and at or near the heart of that holy work is the preaching of the gospel of Jesus Christ.

So what if we can return for help to Phillips Brooks's great definition of preaching as the merger of truth and personality. Truth can be taken as representative of the Bible, of Christian history, of

God's unending presence in our world—truth is the presence of the Holy Spirit in every event of preaching. As Brooks says, without that truth, energized and motivated by the Spirit of God, what takes place is not Christian preaching. When we stand to preach, and when our preaching is based on biblical text, then the Holy Spirit, as paraclete, stands beside us as we preach.

It does even more than that. It not only stands alongside us as we preach; it also moves among those who give themselves to sharing in what we are saying and how we are saying it. It stands alongside every single person in the worship service and experience. The Holy Spirit is there with us all. It is God's holy presence that charges our words, our actions, our mannerisms, our minds and hearts, that energizes the very atmosphere where we have gathered for worship and preaching. Without the Holy Spirit, we cannot preach. We may stand and speak, but without the biblical message that can be honored by the Holy Spirit's presence alongside us, the preaching of the gospel has not taken place.

Just as we emphasize this, however, it is equally important to confront the other side of the coin, the other half of Brooks's equation. As Brooks put it, preaching is only preaching when it is "truth through personality." If truth represents the Holy Spirit's presence in the event of the sermon, personality represents the *preacher's* contribution to the reality and fullness of the event. Personality represents the very best of what we can understand as the preacher's spirit.

This is the *human spirit*. This is not the Holy Spirit, God's Spirit, which can be, and is, poured out on all of those who call upon God's name, the one that energizes for life eternal. *Personality* is the spirit that comes upon every single human being by virtue of our being created in the image of God. This is who we are, with God, as Genesis puts it, having blown into our nostrils the breath of life so that we have become living souls. Every human being possesses personality; and, as we gradually come to know only too well, personalities are like fingerprints—it appears that of the billions and billions of people who live now or have lived on the earth *no two of us are, or ever have been, exactly alike.*

The act of preaching is an act of human personality, of human spirit. No two preachers ever preach alike, nor can they, since no two personalities are ever alike. It is in the improvisational mode of preaching in which the preacher's personality makes its own most powerful contribution to the gospel of Christ. Strong personalities belong in the pulpit. Personalities that are vivid, even sometimes quirky, can be exciting in the pulpit. Personalities are not to be *hidden* in the pulpit; instead, they are to stand tall and unique and vibrant—living souls speaking from their—our—own depths.

Personality is not the same as ego—that has to be said, too. Ego is a conscious thing, showing itself off. One would like to say that it is not a danger in the pulpit, but it always is. Ego is a puffed-up caricature of one's personality. When *personality* is allowed to be itself, it is unself-conscious. Personality is not excessively overbearing about anything. It is an individual who is not acting, who is not trying to be something. It is a person who becomes so caught up in the message being spoken that he or she forgets himself or herself and just *is*—that is when a unique human personality receives its freest and most compelling expression.

The point is a simple one—and one on which we conclude. It is that, by God's own design, the two great spirits of the universe, each a result of the Creator's plan and power, come together whenever a preacher moves before people in the act of preaching. When the gospel of Holy Scripture is preached, the Spirit of God is active and moving, sharper than that proverbial two-edged sword. Divine Spirit can take the preacher's struggling words and ideas and emotions and use them to articulate the priceless message of salvation and sacred living to expectant people.

That Spirit of God, however, cannot do its work without the full-fledged participation of the holy *human* spirit that arises from the preacher's own unique personality. People are drawn to human personality—there are no two ways about that. When this becomes distorted, it results in a cult of celebrity, and such cults are often devastating siren songs for preachers of extraordinary personality. At the same time, preachers must let their personalities shine through their preaching, knowing that while the Holy Spirit is alive and active, so is the preacher's own distinctive human spirit. Without truth, there is no preaching—that we know. What we also must not forget is that without the power of the preacher's personality, there is no preaching either. In the pulpit, those two great spirits meet in a God-ordained process of power and glory.

Notes

1. John S. McClure, Ronald J. Allen, Dale P. Andrews, L. Susan Bond, Dan P. Moseley, and G. Lee Ramsey Jr., *Listening to Listeners: Homiletical Case Studies* (St. Louis: Chalice Press, 2004), 172-73.

2. Phillips Brooks, *Lectures on Preaching* (New York: E. P. Dutton & Co., 1877), 5. The lectures can now be found in several editions, and under different names; but reading them in an original edition is still the most interesting thing to do. For years, they were known only as the *Lectures on Preaching*.